FUTURE
LIVES

FUTURE LIVES

a fearless guide to our transition times

J. L. SIMMONS

BEAR & COMPANY
PUBLISHING
SANTA FE, NEW MEXICO

LIBRARY OF CONGRESS CATALOGING-IN-PUBLICATION DATA

Simmons, J.L. (Jerry Laird), 1933-
    Future lives: a fearless guide to our transition times / by
J.L. Simmons.
        p. cm.
    Includes bibliographical references.
    ISBN 0-939680-76-9
        1. Social history—20th century.   2. Social prediction.
    3. Civilization, Modern.   I. Title.
    HN18.S548   1990
    303.49—dc20   90-65
                                                    CIP

Copyright © 1990 by J.L. Simmons, Ph.D.

Bear & Company, Inc.
Santa Fe, NM 87504-2860

Cover photo: Wernher Krutein
Cover & interior design: Kathleen Katz
Editing: Gail Vivino
Typography: Casa Sin Nombre, Ltd.
Printed in the United States of America by R.R. Donnelley

9 8 7 6 5 4 3 2 1

'Tis not too late to seek a better world.

ALFRED, LORD TENNYSON

CONTENTS

ACKNOWLEDGMENTS

Gratitude to my loving editors, Nola Simmons, Barbara Hand Clow, and Gail Vivino. And my appreciation for all the Bear & Company clan who are working to make a kinder and gentler world for real.

In a thousand multidimensional ways, my companion, Nola Simmons, has contributed to this book and my present life. The ripples spread out endlessly from her contributions.

I also express my gratitude to all the human beings I have known in this life—friends, relatives, acquaintances, lovers, adversaries. You have all been my teachers, providing soul mirrors for my own evolvement.

And finally a secret acknowledgment to my age-old comrades-at-arms. It's been a long walk, but the Force is with us now.

PROLOGUE
The Secret

There is a secret that I very much want to share with you in this book. It is an open secret but it is still not particularly well known. All too often it gets lost amidst an avalanche of alarming news stories and contagious negative images that abound in our mass media.

This secret is hardly ever mentioned in the popular media, hardly ever taken into account by government task forces or committees, and often not even acknowledged by the rest of us. The secret is simple to state but sometimes difficult to fully grasp and believe, although it is almost endless in its enchanting implications for our present and future lives.

What is this secret? It is simply that we, *Homo sapiens*, are doing rather well, even though we've so often been told otherwise. For instance, we human beings have, so far in our history, accomplished a great many things that we can all be very proud of. Furthermore, although we have very real problems to handle, we are in a much better position to handle them than we have ever been before. The possibilities that are opening up for our near and distant future lives are breathtaking. The prospects for the future encompass and exceed many of our wildest dreams.

I know—it might be a startling idea that we should be very proud of our humanness and that our past, present, and future are more light than dark. But if you step back from the parade of wranglings and woes that pass for "The News" and instead focus on the deeper evolutionary history of our individual and collective journeys on this planet, a different picture from the one presented by the media begins to emerge. Where we've been, where we are now, and where we're going all get very interesting. This picture restores a spirit of adventure to the human story.

It has become a well-worn cliche to say that we are pres-

ently in a "cusp" time—a time of major transition from
something to *something else.* The times are a'changing. In
fact there are a host of factors loose in the world today that are
brand new in human history. When we contemplate this
cliche, get inside it, and start to gather the truths that surround it, a wonderful and fascinating story emerges that is *our
story.*

It is not helpful to be too left brain, or intellectual, about
our story, because bare numbers and trend lines represent a
living tapestry of interwoven beings who cry and laugh and
sulk and sing. To capture something of this aliveness, the
cliche needs to be stretched in two directions. First, it needs to
be stretched and expanded historically to encompass our past,
present, and possible future. With such a "long view," we can
make much more sense out of what's going on. Second, it
needs to be expanded so that our conception of the nature of
human beings encompasses much more spiritual depth and
height. When we carry out these two expansions, our story
becomes multidimensional. Then we can come to understand
much more about what's *really* happening now and about
what will probably happen in the future. For all our temporary tumults and tragedies, which are also very real, our
story is a positive and heartening one. Also, there *can* be
happy endings.

In order for us to dive beneath the surface manifestations
and go for "the longer view," we need to combine left-brain
analytical thinking with right-brain intuitive projections.
Either brain hemisphere alone is impoverished, but together
they can do a complete job, just as both hands together can
do things that neither hand can do alone.

Something truly incredible is happening before our very
eyes. The whole world around us is changing, and we are at
the beginning of a new historical spiral that will be as unlike
our recent past as our present lifestyles are unlike those of the
early hunters and gatherers. Few people have been in a posi-

tion to grasp the full scope of this metamorphosis be
they have not had all the facts about it, although a great m
people have already intuitively sensed it. History is at a
threshold. Whatever your feelings, whatever your persuasions,
whatever your hopes and dreams, these changes are surely
worth knowing about.

The more we know and understand about these current
transitions, the more conscious our actions can be. We can, as
the visionary priest Teilhard de Chardin pointed out, be conscious architects of our own evolution. Predictions about the
future have frequently failed because they did not take into
account the *free will* of the beings who are continuously shaping and reshaping it. The social scientist H.W. Smith, in his
book, *Social Psychology*, has assembled a great many studies
documenting the numerous ways in which humans have free
will or "degrees of freedom" in their daily living. Because of
free will, our future is open to our own artistry.

So this book is also about our increasing freedom. There
are many creatures who languish and die in captivity, and I've
long suspected that human beings are among them.

Looking over our present transition times, many people
might feel that it is naively and innocently optimistic to talk
about the good things going on and the grand possibilities of
our future lives. However, there are legions of facts and trends
to back up a positive outlook without denying the real difficulties we face.

Even if a situation is grim, there's no sense being grim about
it. Even if things do turn out badly for a while, it is probably true
that, to paraphrase a famous one-liner, the pessimist suffers a
thousand calamities, the optimist but one—or none.

Part One
TRANSITION TIMES

We are in an epoch for which we have no precedent in history.

GEORGE TREVELYAN

I believe I've found the missing link between animal and civilized man. It is us.

KONRAD LORENZ

They asked Buddha what time it was and he said, "Now!"

Chapter 1

BAD NEWS & GOOD NEWS

There is a grave distortion in our worldwide communications network that serves humanity very badly and leads us to believe that the world is a far darker and more dangerous place than it actually is. Let me show you how this distortion works and you can judge for yourself.

When my family and I lived in Los Angeles a few years back, the children's grandparents constantly worried about whether we had been shot, raped, or washed into the sea. They were almost continuously alarmed because of the "news" coverage of the West Coast they watched every evening. Meanwhile, my family and I were carrying on a pleasant and exciting California lifestyle. We had our difficulties to be sure, but they never appeared on the evening news. Also, the stories on the evening news portrayed situations we never ran into. The good things happening in people's lives were almost never aired. In other words, the media were creating *distorted images* of West Coast living.

Let me explain this another way. I did some estimates for a large midwestern metropolitan area, and this is what I came up with:

• Yesterday someone was brutally murdered; but half a million people found a new friend.

- One person was taken hostage; but several thousand people enjoyed foreign sights and some rest and revitalization.

- The day before yesterday, sixty people were killed in a plane crash; but two million people successfully reached their destinations.

- A celebrity was heartbroken; but half a million people found love.

- A few dozen people hurt others badly; but many thousands of people helped others greatly.

- Someone died of food poisoning; but over a hundred million Americans enjoyed the pleasure and brief respite of eating a tasty lunch.

And so on.

In truth there *are* real tragedies occurring every day, but we need to look at the ratio of good events to bad events, which is sometimes *a million or more to one*.

We should all certainly take some precautions in life, much like slipping on a jacket if it is chilly outside. A woman is foolish to wander the streets alone at three in the morning; anyone is foolish to drive home with a drunken friend; and mail order investments do not give you something for nothing. However, it is a matter of *odds*. The headlines miss the fact that, with a precaution or two, the odds are overwhelmingly in our favor. Even more importantly, we have individually and collectively proven our abilities, again and again, *to change the odds* to further favor the outcomes we desire.

I have gone through over three hundred articles about our transition times, most in major publications or scholarly journals, and most by experts in some specialty—many by famous names. I did an informal analysis of them, distilling their basic data and messages. With some wonderful exceptions, the overwhelming majority were negative and alarming, with perhaps a consolation or two thrown in. Most of them failed to recognize the deeper historical trends. For instance, some articles spoke of the "mid-life crisis" without noting that for the first time in history the majority of the populace *even lives* to the age of mid-life. As another example, there was much concern in the articles about the problems in our schools, with no mention of the fact that for the first time ever in history most humans are *receiving* some formal education. In my opinion, mid-life problems and education troubles are much preferable to a thirty-year lifespan and no education. The articles mostly missed the stupendous accomplishments of human beings as a sentient race on planet Earth. They also confirmed what I had suspected: that the conventional social sciences had become somewhat dreary.

If the messages of these articles were all the truth there is, we would be justified in embracing despair or nihilism. But they are not the full truth. They missed most of the good news, the brighter possibilities for our now and future lives.

This negativity tends to "generalize" in people's minds. We hear about an Internal Revenue Service conviction and begin to vaguely dread an audit. We see pictures of a single train wreck and pick up a little fear about traveling. We see flutters in economic trends and become anxious about our own job security. If we lived entirely isolated lives and only knew about the outside world through media news coverage, we would think it was a terrible place of unrelieved miseries and disasters.

The media news and the three hundred articles are examples of "negative affirmations"—negative mass thought forms that keep current populations needlessly agitated and alarmed. Since they produce distressed behavior, these negative images are sometimes needlessly self-fulfilling. They are a heavy invalidation of our real accomplishments and so can lead us astray. It is insightful to think of these mass thought-forms as *spells* over the land and its people. They paint a dangerous environment and cut people's reach into it, making us timorous (and sometimes tumorous). Also, they deal almost exclusively with only the most superficial level of historical change, as we will see.

In *The Evolutionary Journey,* the eminent futurist Barbara Marx Hubbard put the point nicely: "We have examined in current times, with great perception, the possibility of unprecedented breakdown. But we have not examined with equal care the possibility of unprecedented breakthrough."

*   *   *

There is another pervasive distortion in our mass communications network that is starting to fade but is still problematic. It results from knowledge lags and other factors that I'll discuss later in the book. It is that real-life situations and difficulties are often left undiscussed while reports of superficial events flood the airways and tabloids. For instance, the current medical situation in the United States is such that it bankrupts far more people than a dip in the stock market. (Half the personal bankruptcies in the United States are caused by high medical bills.) As another example, drunk driving is far more dangerous, and ruins more lives per year, than all the terrorists in the world combined. You probably don't know anyone killed or abused by terrorists, but you almost certainly know someone killed or maimed in a drunk-driving accident. Coverage of the superficial and the sensational produces a distortion in people's perceptions of the real social problems we may be facing, which we should be addressing for our own good. For example, it would be wise to concern ourselves more with the environmental crisis than with the private lives of celebrities and politicians. The extent of these bad news distortions may perhaps more easily be seen by comparing them with more typical real-life situations.

When I have been out in the world doing field research, I

have often been astonished by the *abilities* of ordinary people to adapt and cope successfully, and to build something of their lives—whatever the circumstances and whatever changes came down upon them. These abilities were not incorporated into most of the theories about human nature I learned as a graduate student. I have seen people wrestle with disappointments, crises, and traumas. I have seen them suffer. But I have also seen them eventually transcend their situations by rising to the occasion. I have sometimes suspected that such abilities are the greatest resource we possess as a race.

I have gone out and asked people, "What's happening that's good?" Some of them were really taken aback by the rephrasing of the common question "What's happening?" I could see some people change their focus of attention right at that moment. Then a whole book full of good things came pouring out of them.

The bias toward negativity also exists in our fields of entertainment. Consider that someone submits a television script or novel about Jack and Jill. These two main characters meet, enjoy falling in love, become happily married, have two healthy fun kids, and lead a good life. Probably no one would buy this story because it lacks "plot" and "drama." Yet hundreds of millions of people have lived this script, and hundreds of millions more yearn to do so. (Some sit-com ratings show that people *do* like happy stories.)

So far, every human civilization has had both positive and negative collective images or mass thoughtforms floating about within it. The media can mislead us because of their distorted emphasis. These negative distortions actively empower the more negative mass images in the culture, which then can lead to self-fulfilling consequences such as the hysterical buildup of mistrust between nations. This is partly the source of so many gloom-and-doom scenarios during the last half century—scenarios far bleaker than most of the things that have actually occurred. This may also be the intuitive source of the whimsical folk saying "No news is good news." The surface news is bad and alarming, but as we look deeper and wider, the bottom lines are good and the picture gets brighter and brighter.

Another point: "The News" certainly does not cover all that is really going on in the world by any stretch. A great many visionary writers have depicted the interpenetrating spiritual events happening throughout the physical plane that are not even hinted at on the six o'clock news. For the general public, this amounts to "hidden stories." As Sanaya Roman, the famous channeler of the discarnate entity Orin, has said, "Many highly evolved souls with much important work to do choose to do it anonymously." Those who follow the mass media may be "informed," but not well informed.

In many cases, reporters know little or nothing about the subjects they are reporting on. In their innocence, they often serve merely as unwitting conduits for the press releases of special-interest groups and political figures. In their book *Manufacturing Consent*, Herman and Chomsky document how the mass media largely serve and promote the vested interests and ideologies of the privileged groups in our society. You can test these biases for yourself. Pick a subject you are personally knowledgeable about. Then read a couple of mass-media articles on it or watch a television special report about it. You will see how much information really gets left out. We often have to go outside the regular channels to get the real news of the world.

Beyond the news inputs, there is the matter of our own emotional positioning. I know some people who are convinced that the world is about to experience disaster. This position deeply colors their lives. They are wracked with forebodings, dour anxieties, and down-in-the-mouth emotions. This position distorts all of their relationships, perceptions, plans, hopes, and dreams. They are suffering right now, no matter what happens in the future.

I know other people who are optimistic. They feel things might come out all right. Meanwhile, they build their lives, enjoy their coffee and companions, their hobbies, their pets, and their television favorites. Even if disaster does fall, they seem more likely to come through it.

You choose.

Chapter 2

THE CHANGING

T imes are changing.

Some people might ask, "What's this got to do with me?" Well, here's the answer and it's a crucial one—the stuff that our lives are made of.

Biologists, ecologists, and social scientists have been busy scientifically documenting what mystics have been claiming for millennia—that each individual human *exists within a dense web* of relationships, groups, organizations, societies, planetary systems, and higher dimensions. For each individual, this web tendrils out endlessly in every imaginable direction. In joy or sorrow, we are all braided together. As Barbara Marx Hubbard has said, "Whatever happens, happens to us all."

As one example, sociologist Stanley Milgram's networking research demonstrated that each person in the United States is, on the average, only six or eight interpersonal links from every other person in the country. That is, you know somebody who knows somebody. . .who knows the president, or a current rock star, or anyone. And there's a small girl in, say, Alabama who knows someone, who knows someone. . .who knows you.

It is estimated that less than ten more links would carry this phenomenon to any single individual on the globe.

17

Therefore, there is a "weak" interpersonal network *linking together every person living on the planet today.*

When you help any part of this network, you are simultaneously helping yourself; when you diminish any part of it, you are diminishing and impoverishing yourself. This is one way in which we all have a direct hand in helping to paint our own skies blue or gray.

When, in addition to individuals, all the groups and organizations and societies and so forth are included, it is apparent how dense and intertwined this web really is. No matter how alone and isolated a person may feel, no matter how few direct social contacts they may presently have, this dense web is continuously operating in countless ways.

A while ago, when I was living a quiet life, I became personally curious about this interlocking web, so I checked it out. On an ordinary working day I found myself interfacing with no less than twenty-six organizations on levels ranging from local to planetary to "astral." When I traced out a few strands of my own interpersonal network of first-name-basis acquaintances, I was astounded. I was three links away from rock musician Bruce Springsteen and the governor of the state; I was four links from ex-president Carter and then-president Reagan. I was four links away from television host Johnny Carson, five links from England's Princess Diana, and seven links from the Emperor Hirohito of Japan. I was also only four links away from the murderous former cult leader Charles Manson. How many links would I be from, say, a goat herder in the hills of Pakistan? And I'm not even a gregarious person.

C. Wright Mills, the maverick social scientist, pointed out that people usually have difficulty realizing the linkages between their own personal biographies and the intertwining web of social forces and conditions. For instance, social problems such as environmental pollution or drunk driving often don't get *real* for people until they are personally touched by them. The lives of individuals cannot be fully understood without some understanding of the web.

The strands and levels of this web generate the very fabric of social reality for their members, the blueprints for their social lives. These web strands are so much a part of what most people mean when they say "reality" and they are so thoroughly socialized into the very thoughts, habits, and emotional responses of their participants that they become the "field" within which personal games are played out. However, awareness of them is generally quite low. Their influence is so pervasive that they are simply part of "the way things are" to most people.

The parts of this web are highly interrelated, but we are only beginning to become aware of this. The fact is, however, that, even on the physiological level, people will wilt or bloom depending on their "climate"—the barriers and opportunities and energy fields provided by the web existing in a particular historical spiral. This is the source of the concepts of socio-somatic disorders and socio-psychological influences.

What "times are changing" really means is that the web is changing:

1. Its forms, quality, and nature are changing.
2. It is becoming even more dense and interconnected, but also more fluid and flexible.
3. It is manifesting greater consciousness and self-awareness on the part of its individual members.

A few centuries ago, sailors might have built a fire on a beach of a South Pacific island; this might not have meant very much to the rest of the world. Not so today. Today, none of us can ignore the South Pacific or Portugal or anywhere else on the planet. Nowadays, most of us are involved with a vast number of organizations of which we are not even members. Their activities and products come swooping into our lives with our morning coffee or noon mail. Meanwhile, our individual activities and products go rippling back outward over the entire globe.

As the noted British spiritual teacher George Trevelyan has said in *A Vision of the Aquarian Age,* "We are in an epoch for which we have no precedent in history." In *The Global Brain,* Peter Russell, the visionary physicist, similarly pointed out, "Few of us can fully grasp just how fast things are changing."

Human populations have always been quite ambivalent about social change, both hoping for the changes that will improve their lot and at the same time dreading the changes that might shatter the arrangements they are living by and maybe plunge them into a chaos of unpredictability and shock. There is more freedom on the one hand, more chaos on the other.

There are, of course, many different kinds of change. Exponential growth is one extreme kind of change, shattering cataclysm is another. Mathematically, there are an infinite number of curves that depict the shape of different sorts of change. We talk about change, both personally and collectively, in hopes of doing a better job of anticipating it. There are smooth, benign curves of change, and there are convulsive, destructive ones. The major historical changes have not been linear progressions; they have been more like bloomings.

Change is the prevailing mode of the living universe. Change is sensuous. It involves skin feelings and deep inner feelings, glands, bile, buoyant sensations, and aching heads. It is not just some abstract thing. Change can lift you up or cast you down. Change can be kind of scary.

There are sometimes casualties of change. But there are also casualties of things remaining the same. There are, for example, people who feel they cannot put up with another year of their lives as they now are.

Some people experience difficulties and tragedies during

times of change. But such difficulties befall people during *any* historical time period, whether there is change or not. *Positive changes* can significantly lower these casualty rates. For example, the massive changes created by the Industrial Spiral have eventuated in longer, better lives for the majority of people living in nations that have gone through them. Today the average person lives better and longer, and has more leisure time, than even the gentry of previous centuries. In most modern nations, even today's lower classes are in most ways much better off than the poverty classes of earlier times and places. They eat better, live longer, and have more chances to escape their lot. There has been massive upward mobility for hundreds of millions of humans during the last century. So we've collectively accomplished a great deal. The stark conditions among Native Americans and in many Third World countries warn us, however, that there is still much to accomplish.

The changes currently transpiring are usually described as a transformation from the old world to a new era. Some sectors of the populace say this is good, some say it is bad, but most agree that it *is* occurring. We need to leave the moral judgments aside for the moment and look more deeply at this. There are three levels of change going on.

First, there is the superficial level of changes, such as in world stock markets, the value of the U.S. dollar, election results, and the widespread use of video cassette recorders. This level is visible to most people (including officials) and has much public focus on it. The changes at this level preoccupy our newspeople and our committees, yet these events are really only *symptoms* of the deeper shifts occurring.

Second, there are the shifts in societal and planetary infrastructures. These include trends in major social institutions such as the recent emergence of the two-income family, the introduction of mass education, and the rise of Japan as a world technological and economic power. These trends are often studied and cogently discussed by experts in specialized fields. Sometimes the data on these trends is incorporated into progressive college courses and quoted as "filler items" in newspapers and magazines. For instance, it is well known by experts within relevant fields that America has changed from being the largest creditor nation to the largest debtor nation, and that the U.S. tax structure is skewed in favor of the rich. As another example of this second level, it is known that the proportion of counselors who have broken with conventional psychology and who now practice alternative techniques such as reality therapy or past-life regression has rapidly increased in the last two decades.

Underneath these two levels of change is the third and deepest level—that of vast historical social tides. These include changes such as the progressive urbanization and modernization of the world, humanity's steadily increasing intervention in the natural environment for good and for ill, the loosening of the bonds of tradition, and the world emergence into a post-industrial social order. We are only beginning to understand these very deep kinds of shifts. Much of humanity is not even aware of them.

This third level is the strongest level in that the other two are superstructures floating upon it. *This third level holds the most promise for us.* It is the level least talked about, but the one providing the raw materials for the future lives we are building, and the level where our best hopes lie.

Ordinary people and media commentators often get caught up in the first level. They get lost among the individual trees and don't see the forest. The second level is often the arena of reformers, critics, and special-interest-group conflicts. Beyond this, astute observers and scholars, as well as those gifted with an unusual degree of intuition, have often known about the third, or deepest, tidal level. However, these people have rarely been listened to by decision makers, the business world, or most of the populace. The tidal shifts occur anyway.

We can indirectly gauge major changes at this deepest level by examining statistical trends and opinion polls. These reflect changes in lifestyles and collective thoughtforms. For example, the emergence of post-industrial society is indicated by the steady drop in the proportion of people engaged in agriculture and industry, and the steady rise in the proportion of people engaged in information or service jobs. The loosening of rigid traditions is indicated by the fact that, in the last fifty years, the fraction of Americans who would vote for a woman president has risen from around one-third to over four-fifths.

Changes bring new problems, new experiences, and new opportunities. On the whole, many people have not yet learned to handle change very well. Minor changes can be adjusted to, but massive changes are likely to be at least temporarily upsetting. Major historical changes are almost always a *surprise* to those experiencing them. People don't usually "see them coming." If that weren't enough, many people find that the changes violate some of their deep moral values. They see such things as easy divorce laws, R-rated entertainment, and the growth of mystic spirituality as corruption and decay, even though others see these changes as liberating.

During the periods when massive change is occurring, large numbers of people are left with culture lag and future shock. These people were raised and socialized in a different time period, which is now gone. For them many things, from the family to music to investments and careers, just don't work the same way anymore. This is why they often feel that everything is going to hell, when actually it is just changing. These people may even join backlash movements against some of the changes because they do not feel at home in the present circumstances, not realizing that the new era and the good news is for them, too.

Historically, organizations and societies have handled major changes even more badly than individuals. Their operating patterns are usually set up to handle more of the same thing, or changes that occur in gradual, straight-line graph trends. Their patterns are usually more "set in place" and less flexible than those of individuals. Real changes catch them unaware, and the result is that they frequently deteriorate or shatter instead of creatively adapting to the new situations. However, this, too, is changing as evolution on all levels becomes more conscious and self-conscious, as Peter Russell has noted. Organizations and societies can also win.

To make some sense out of the legions of facts and trends and hunches and opinions swirling around at this time, it is useful to find some bottom lines and pursue their implications. Here are some of the bottom lines:

1. We—the current population of the planet—are the transition people, living in transition times. We are first-generation immigrants into the new era. Depending on our individual mindsets, heart-sets, and spirit-sets, this makes us either explorers and adventurers or displaced persons.

2. We are coming into a new, "never before," emergent evolutionary level of social order. There are resonances with past eras, but we are on the threshold of a qualitatively new historical spiral.

3. We are intervening in our environment both creatively and destructively to an unprecedented degree. We are building new environments, such as lighted, heated, and cooled buildings, and soon a permanent space station. With this acceleration, both the promises and the threats increase manyfold.

4. There has been a massive loosening of the ties that have historically bound people. This has meant a stupendous increase in individual freedoms. The predetermining powers of social class, gender, age, and tribe are fading, although still visible. We are freer than ever before to make

our own individual choices. A larger percentage of the populace than ever before is therefore directly involved in shaping society.

5. Gross imbalances in deep polarities such as male / female, self-interest / collective-interest, and materialism / spirituality, which have held sway for many centuries, are starting to rebalance and integrate. The importance of this integrating process cannot be overestimated.

6. Change is becoming the norm. For instance, fashion is frequently replacing custom. We are learning to live with change, which makes each change smoother and more positive.

7. The facts of our lives have shifted, almost while we weren't looking, and they are continuing to shift. These shifts often show up in statistics such as the percentage of two-income families, the average age of the populace, the movement of the labor force into new careers, or the percent of women gainfully employed. They also show up in world overpopulation figures and in the number of trees lost each day. Behind these statistics are raw truths directly affecting our personal lives and future histories.

8. The whole world is becoming more urban and more "modern." This entails leaving behind the way most people have historically lived. This change represents a *basic* shift in human lifestyle.

9. Most of us don't really know what we're doing in handling the transition or in attempting to midwife the birth of the new era. Unintended consequences abound, and we are innocents abroad. We are sometimes misled because we don't recognize what is new. As long as we *know* that we don't know what we're doing, however, we are on the right path.

10. A new level of consciousness is emerging on our planet. This consciousness is larger than its components; it is big-

ger than the New Age or the "Aquarian Conspiracy" or the human-potential movement or Amnesty International, although each of these is a part of it. It includes rising expectations, increases in the level of what is unacceptable, and all the myriad forms of self-realization. It can be glimpsed in such diverse things as the "thawing" of Russia, the worldwide condemnation of apartheid, the laws against marital rape, the high-frontier and space-colony advocate societies, and the rapidly growing concern about the environment. It encompasses many odd bedfellows, some of whom perhaps don't presently even like each other, but who share the utterly fundamental attribute of raised consciousness. Because of this consciousness, our planet will never be the same again.

Chapter 3

HISTORICAL TIDES

For beings on planet Earth, evolvement is both individual and collective. There is now ample evidence to back up the claim that an evolutionary sweep has been occurring in human history. This evolution is *not* an example of Darwinian survival of the fittest. Rather, it represents the continual emergence of humanity at higher and higher levels of individual and collective organization, awareness, and accomplishment. This development is also not linear (straight line) but *spiral*, complete with some twists. Each new stage builds upon all the developments of the previous stages. This ascending spiral, as it manifests, is the third, deepest level of social change mentioned in the previous chapter.

The conditions we experience in our current transitional times have not appeared full blown from nowhere. This current era rests upon the platform of developments in earlier spirals, and we are presently, collectively, building the platform upon which the upcoming spiral will rest.

Historically, each new spiral has involved a qualitative transformation of the lives of its people. Succeeding spirals are not just simple expansions of preexisting conditions. *Each spiral is qualitatively different.* In fact, the spirals are so different that the conditions prevailing in any particular one would be

27

utterly unbelievable to the people inhabiting the one before it.

When a spiral is established and in full swing, its patterns and lifestyles *prevail.* That is, they are experienced by the overwhelming majority of the populace. Also, the character of the spiral is reflected in its dominant belief structures and institutions. Different life chances, different games and constraints and opportunities prevail in different spirals. Most of the populace take the prevailing conditions of their spiral for granted as "the way things are."

Each new spiral has therefore involved stupendous changes in the way people have lived. Sometimes these changes have been called "good," sometimes "bad," but in most cases these judgments have been a reflection of fixed ideas and local moral traditions rather than a cool examination of the changes. This is still true today.

Each transition to a new spiral has been tumultuous. Especially in its early stages, each spiral has also contained abuses. *But each new spiral has been an uplifting.* Each has had its pathfinders and pioneers—and its laggards. Each has had its potentials, some of which have been realized and some of which are yet to be fully realized. As each has emerged, it has contained a great many surprises for the people living through it.

There have always been rises and falls of particular groups, as well as many other developments, within the broad span of each spiral—each has had its own history. The prevailing forms of a spiral have had different "flavors" in different geographic locales, colored by local customs and circumstances. For instance, the "Hunting and Gathering Spiral" was colored by different local circumstances in Africa from those on the North American plains. There have always been minor local variations in each spiral, and no doubt in future centuries there will be local color differences between different space colonies. However, the overall character of each particular spiral puts its unmistakable stamp on all the locales within its bounds.

Each spiral involves a major paradigm shift in the prevailing forms of consciousness. So, a spiral is not just an external, technical thing; it is also deeply reflected in the inner lives and psyches of its people. In addition to the primary form of consciousness, other forms of consciousness are always present in each spiral, but only as minority themes. Among these minority themes are the forerunners of future spirals, as well as themes still manifesting from earlier spirals.

During any spiral there are resonances with similar historical points of earlier, lower spirals. For example, there are certain echoes of Roman times in our present era. This is where the idea that history repeats itself comes from. *But history does not repeat itself.* Each spiral is a higher octave of the previous one, although some notes may resonate with the past. Note that this process is the opposite of entropy. Entropy involves an inexorable decay of systems, while historical spirals involve an inexorable evolvement into higher, more complex systems.

These spirals are, of course, not the whole story. There are other strands that have affected human history: influences from advanced spirits, extraterrestrials, "strays," and eerie transcendental local cultures that have been the stuff of myth. But these anomalies are the subject of another book. My focus here is on the adventures and misadventures of the bulk of humanity.

We can gain more of a feeling of how spirals manifest and where we ourselves may be heading if we take a brief look at several. We can also catch something of the rhythm of progression.

Most early humans lived in the Hunting and Gathering Spiral. They were very much in and with nature—in tune with the natural rhythms of the Earth. They were also routinely aware of the intermingling of the natural and the supernatural, the supernatural consisting of the spirits of nature and animals. Their lives were very precarious, and these people could only gather in small bands, within which there was little organization. They lived on the edge, and even minor setbacks like droughts or contagious illnesses could be disastrous. Also, by and large, they could only collect and own what they could personally carry. To get a feel for this, imagine selecting from all your possessions, clothing, and food only as much as you can personally carry and leaving everything else behind—subsisting from that point on with only what you are carrying and what you can find.

On the next spiral up, the "Gardening and Herding Spiral," humans learned to domesticate animals and plants, and a new historical era dawned. Food supplies became more stable and dependable. Beasts of burden greatly increased the number of things people could possess. There was room for more clothing, more tools, extra food, and tents for better insulation from environmental extremes. There was a bit more leisure time. Somewhat larger human groupings such as the tribe were now possible. There was a bit more time to specialize in certain skills such as tent making. Daily living became less rudimentary, and more elaborate mythologies began to be formed and passed down through the generations orally.

The next spiral, the "Agricultural Spiral," involved the rise and rapid spread of agriculture. It would remain the predominant lifestyle for several thousand years. This spiral produced a far greater surplus of food and wealth above and beyond the subsistence level, and allowed for the growth of permanent settlements and the accumulation of goods. The rise of true cities happened at this time, and it is no accident that the words "city" and "civilization" have the same roots. Central governments that administered large areas arose. There was a new stage that could have enriched many lives, and did greatly enrich a few. There was usually a rigid social order, and the populace was sharply divided into castes. The

privileged class fraction, living on top of the rest, acquired leisure time and many resources. There was a new emergent level
of social organization and a swift increase in full-time
specializations, including craftspeople, priesthoods, and
other quasi-mystic orders. There was increased human mobility through trade and military ventures, which led to a greater
intermingling of customs, religious doctrines, and technologies. Written language, a huge leap forward, appeared. However, these kinds of things were confined almost entirely to
the upper strata and their entourage. The stark class inequalities of this era would be utterly unacceptable in any modernized nation of today.

The next upward spiral, the "Industrial Spiral," was trig-
gered by the Industrial Revolution. This spiral involved a tremendous proliferation of goods and services, a rapid growth
in specialization (like the specialization of cells in complex
organisms), and a great increase in human mobility. Prior to
the Industrial Revolution most people had spent their entire
lives within a tiny ecological and psychic niche, and had been
very little concerned with what went on outside of it unless
the great outside threatened their nests. For every Ulysses or
Marco Polo, there had been a hundred thousand physical and
mental stay-at-homes. The Industrial Spiral began to rapidly
change this situation, and the forms of mobility it engendered are still increasing today.

During the Agricultural Spiral, the prevailing idea was
that humans *supervised* nature. In the Industrial Spiral, the
idea emerged that humans were to *master* nature. Phrases
such as "the conquest of nature" and "taming the wilderness" became cliches arrogantly and triumphantly spoken by
philosophers and great merchant companies alike. This was a
fundamental shift in human attitude toward the planet that
has had numberless positive and negative consequences. This
attitude has enriched lives, but it has also created many
human-made environmental menaces.

A great transformation of the surface of the Earth occurred during the Industrial Spiral, and small cities became giant sprawling metropolises where a growing percentage of the world's population began to live. There was increased freedom along with increased uprootedness, and, for a time, science and rationality were worshiped. God was conceived of as a kind of superaccountant with ledgers and judgment calls about people's worth.

The early days of the Industrial Spiral were quite ragged with mass exploitations both at home and abroad in geographic areas that had not yet uplifted into the spiral. Later, as things became smoother and accommodations among the classes were hammered out, a large proportion of the population found itself with increased goods, services, resources, and leisure. There were more freedoms and more choices available than ever before, and more of the population participated directly in society's culture and infrastructure. As described by the Canadian social theorist Marshall McLuhan, the world, through mass communications and transport, began shrinking toward a "global village." Times had definitely changed.

Not all of the world uplifted to each new spiral as it appeared on the planet, however. In some areas, this was due to lack of opportunity or because the local cultural patterns were too resistive to the necessary changes. Even today, much of the world is still predominantly in the Agricultural Spiral or the Gardening and Herding Spiral. These regions are now, however, rapidly modernizing.

Today, humanity is, as both seers and scientists agree, in transit to the next spiral, which has probably not yet even been properly named. It has been called the "Post-Industrial Society," the "Information Society," the "New Age," the "New Era," and many other things. We may be unable to properly name it yet because we have not yet full experienced it. Can the caterpillar name the butterfly?

However, we can glimpse something of this new spiral's possible outlines. This emerging spiral, like all the others, is a qualitatively new level. For example, people may be working at occupations twenty-five years or so from now that are not even in existence today. Levels of information and technology diffusion from one area of the globe to another are now taking a quantum leap in swiftness and extensiveness. Part 2 will look at many factors of this modern spiral that have never before been experienced by humanity. And there is increased free will in this spiral, sometimes more than we can yet easily handle.

If you contemplate these spirals for a bit, you can begin to see that each successive one holds more potential for an increasing number of people than the previous ones. There is more flexibility, more degrees of freedom, and more fluidity with each succeeding one. This is a relative matter and there are certainly hardships, tragedies, and casualties within each stage, but the direction of succeeding spirals is unmistakably *upward*.

Another interesting thing is that the *rate* of evolution is itself accelerating. The Hunting and Gathering Spiral lasted several hundred thousand years. The span of the Gardening and Herding Spiral was tens of thousands of years. The Agricultural Spiral covered only thousands of years and the Industrial Spiral hundreds of years. Does this mean that the upcoming spiral will be a matter of only decades?

In all of these spirals, there have been mystical and "occult" developments and humans who were in tune with larger spiritual forces. There were always some people who achieved great wisdom and enlightenment. Sometimes these people were important in conventional accounts of history, sometimes not. But in looking at these spirals, I am focusing on the life situations of the vast bulk of humanity, for instance the lives of the *ordinary people* in Egypt (or even Atlantis).

The exceptional people were above and beyond the historical sweeps mentioned so far. They often embodied an intense distillation of some quality inherent in that stage. How much they directly touched the lives of the plodders is another question entirely. More often than not, these exceptional people became the casualties of their times, at least on the physical plane. To focus entirely on such exceptionals and distillations is to manifest our own current individualistic biases.

The role of the exceptionals was often to channel some of the energies, some of the spiritual seeds, involved in the birthing of the era to follow. As a recent example, Albert Einstein certainly belonged more to the upcoming new spiral than to the masses of Detroit factory workers who were his contemporaries during the heyday of industrialism.

Each spiral has presented opportunities of spiritual growth for larger proportions of the populace. However, in each stage such opportunities were partially co-opted and subordinated by humans manifesting coarser-vibration-level desires and zealousness. In each stage there has been a problem of exploitation, in which growth factors in the new spiral have been abused by some to take advantage of others. This reduced the uplifting potential in each case and was something that had to be worked out—usually the hard way— after the transition. In the Hunting and Gathering Spiral, the strongest, cleverest hunter prevailed and when his powers failed he was usually taken out of the game. The Agricultural Spiral, which could have freed most people from immediate survival pressures, was used to establish privileged groups, introduce slavery, embark on military adventures, and so on. The Industrial Spiral, which could have provided relative plenty for all, was partly co-opted by those in favorable positions to grab much of the spoils, establish economic empires, and create huge multinational corporations. Native people stood no chance whatsoever against either technological weaponry or technological economies.

So each previous transmutation has had its dark side. This

is also no doubt true for the upcoming spiral. We may already be seeing the first glimmerings of some of these dark-side characteristics. There are potentials for microwave mind control, technical surveillance as in George Orwell's *1984,* population programming beyond the wildest dreams of earlier despots, telecommunications frauds, thought police, and psychic con games.

The troubles that have dogged each spiral are partly due to the lingering of mass thoughtforms and habit patterns from previous spirals. Fight-or-flight mechanisms are still with us, so we sometimes worry ourselves sick brooding over nonpresent possible threats. There is tribal thinking in our nuclear village. We fear sharing lest we run low ourselves. We still sometimes view humans as cogs in production assembly lines—interchangeable parts. (A bright grad student, for instance, held forth at a faculty gathering how people can find interchangeable spouses if they lose their present ones.) There are widespread drives for mastery and the establishing of pecking orders. These are all parts of our collective and individual karmic heritage, and clearing them is part of our evolvement task.

These heritages have collective karmic implications that we will no doubt discover more fully along the way, because they dog our footsteps. For instance, Hitler was very much a Johnny Come Lately in the genocide game. (Slaughtering other tribes is an ancient practice.) Old images haunt our present transition lives. We still carry a male chauvinist, tribal god thoughtform, a god image of wrath, spitefulness, and petty jealousies who gets off on abject adulation. We had *Gott Mitt Uns* ("God With Us") on the beltbuckles of the storm-troopers.

Like an individual's life-stage passages, the transitions into each higher spiral are tumultuous, often socially convulsive. The changes "reshuffle the deck" of the social order; new roles emerge, priorities shift, values change, and the established status systems are usually scrambled. These things will probably occur again, but each new emerging spiral has always swept into dominance because it has *transcended* the earlier phases.

Echoes of earlier spirals have always remained, but there is never a total collapse or retrogression back to an earlier stage. So today, even if we experience some kind of partial breakdown, history demonstrates that we will not slide backward. The forces producing the successive spirals are evidently too strong and extensive enough to prevent such slides.

There is another factor at work in the evolution of these uplifting spirals. It seems that the human spirit will win out in the long run, however long and tortuous the road, because there are simply too many forces of "Light" in the cosmos for it to be otherwise.

The crucial question before us, then, is, *How smooth or convulsive will the modern transition to a new era be?*

Chapter 4

TRANSITION
PEOPLE

These are the transition times, sandwiched in between the world that has already gone and a new era to come. And we are the transition people living through these times. This state of being in transition is probably the most important underlying fact about our times and our lives. Many of the characteristics, thoughts, feelings, actions, hopes, and fears typical of our times reflect this, and we are *all* involved and embroiled in the transitions, whether we are conscious of it or not.

Most of us would not be comfortable going back and living in the old world of, say, a century ago. We would find much of it stifling and drab, and we would also face more hazards than we might care to. Most of us would not be immediately comfortable in, say, the year 2100 either, because we would probably experience culture shock. We manifest in our *current* incarnations and are creatures of our own times.

The first glimmerings of the characteristics of the upcoming spiral, which could be described as a world community of more awakened humans, are already around us. Interpersonal networks are replacing close-knit extended families; fashion in all things is supplementing custom and rigid traditions; there is a decline of the bonds with our geographic communities and a rise of voluntarily *chosen* affiliations with social communities and subcultures.

The details of our lives are becoming more *voluntary*. Situations are less structured. Our social arrangements are less rigid. Institutions and societies are less ritualized. (What I do this afternoon is mostly up to me.) We are less stuck in the circumstances of our birth or gender or ethnic roots. It is now harder to trap someone or to become trapped ourselves in circumstances. Even our prisons have television, coke machines, training programs, and parole. It is also easier than ever to *change* our circumstances. This alone creates more flexibility and flux in society. The web strands, although more dense and interdependent, are more fluid and flexible than they have ever been before.

Some people feel impatient because the changes are occurring too slowly. Others feel overwhelmed by the speed of change—they feel "motion sickness" and are wistful about the alleged stability of the past. But we're all aboard and on the trip into the future.

There are a host of cliches that could be applied to this situation. "We live in exciting, but challenging times." "We are at a historical crossroads." "The potential for either great achievement or total destruction exists now as never before." "We are at a turning point." "We must change our ways before it's too late." Or, as one sixty-year-old handyman said to me, "We're in deep shit."

A common image is that we have one foot in the old world and one foot in the new. But the old world is already gone and the new era has not yet manifested, so actually we are standing on shifting ground. Even as we try to secure our personal, economic, and social "holdings," the social fabric within which we exist melts and changes again.

There is a fundamental linkage that carries us through this transition. All of us who live within a society are at least to some degree *dependent* upon it. This includes the transcendents and the dropouts, although they may reduce this dependency by learning to live without its package deals and by ceasing to listen so intently to its cajolings and admonitions. However, no one can entirely become one's own dentist, house builder, book publisher, car manufacturer, and money printer. So dropping out or transcending are only relative. The very ground we stand on is ultimately owned by the state. As noted earlier, social critic C. Wright Mills pointed out that people often do not sense the linkages between their own personal biographies and the social forces around them, but the linkages are nevertheless there and very active. Part 2 discusses a great many of these linkages between history and individual lives.

We are flooded with information about our transition times, but how do we get a handle on them so that we might understand the transitions better and gain some notion of where we might be heading? In other words, where are we? And where are we going?

There is a fundamental paradox of our times that constantly touches our lives and every aspect of our social order: we are simultaneously both *more free* and *more adrift* than any people in history have ever been. If you take a good look at the people around you today, you will discover that a good many of them seem to have deeply mixed feelings about themselves and the world. The general picture you will get is that contemporary life is a patchwork of shining accomplishments and promises against a background of anxieties, stresses, and vague threats. Our times are shot through with ironies and paradoxes. People are simultaneously freer but more anxious, better off but more restless, and more educated but more adrift in unknown waters.

Perhaps the greatest irony is that our pains and problems are the backside of some of our greatest collective accomplishments—the things in which we can take the most pride. Most of our "pluses" and "minuses" have arisen from the same historical forces.

The talked-about problems of our times—race relations, international turmoil, crime, the role of women (and men), technology, and so on—are often only surface aspects of the underlying problem of making the transition from the old order to the new emerging world. These problems cannot be solved at the symptomatic level; we have often tried and failed. Many of the agonies and unsettlements of our age may be the growing pains in our transition from the age of "It Is Written" to the age of "What's Happening?" This transition involves a stupendous shift from living by tradition to self-consciously making our way in an ever-shifting and loose-knit social fabric.

Transition people are released or "turned loose" in both larger proportion and more ways than ever before. There has been a progressive meltdown of traditions, and no end to this process is in sight. This meltdown troubles the social waters temporarily, but it is a necessary development if people are to be free enough in the upcoming spiral to *consciously* design their own lives and social orders.

The increasing freedom of modern transition people has resulted from the third, deepest tidal level of change mentioned in chapter 2. Two of the deep changes occurring at this level are the loosening of the structural fabric of societies and the fading of stability and continuity through time. Some people judge these as representing the collapse of civilization, and some herald them as the long-awaited emancipation of human beings on a mass scale.

Contemporary people have been partially released from the physical and psychological bonds of the old order because technology and urbanism have "accidentally" created a more wide-open society. Most people today in technologically advanced countries can slip around the corner and be in a new world; we can hop on a plane and go where no one knows us;

we can go to a drugstore and buy a book that may be high treason and heresy in the eyes of our social circle; we can go to college and learn to see our own upbringing as a set of curious local customs. There may be people who don't like the fact that we can do these things, but, historically speaking, it's too late for them to stop us now. Such things are only the surface manifestations of our greater freedom, anyway. The jubilation of folk singer Bob Dylan's sixties line "Your sons and daughters are beyond your command" is a signpost of our era.

As the old communal and tribal bonds have loosened, the control of individuals through rigid tradition and gossip has given way to a much weaker and much more minimal regulation of the populace through laws and diffuse public opinion. The crucial difference between these two modes is that the first one pushes people into complying with standards of what they "should" do, while the latter merely sets up wide boundaries beyond which people "shouldn't" go, but within which they can do pretty much what they please. Also, people can get away with breaking laws much more easily than they can with breaking taboos. Legislated morality is far weaker and less constricting than morality imposed by ever-watchful kinfolk.

Our present elaborate structures of laws, courts, and enforcement agencies may have arisen as a kind of temporary historical stopgap between the previous reign of "it is written" moral dogma and an upcoming time of individual self-responsibility and self-sufficiency. These modern structures are somewhat biased in favor of privileged groups, both in their form and their administration, but ordinary people are still far freer under them than they were in czarist Russia or ancient Egypt. Because people are usually preoccupied with living on the narrow ledge of the present, it is difficult for them to see these deep trends, but the trends are there and they have been documented.

In previous times, the main consequence of the fact that society was more tightly knit was that its members were

almost forced to comply with local rigid notions of what con-
stituted "a good man," "a good wife," "a pious person," and
so on, for all the different positions and roles in that society.
People had to stuff themselves and their activities into the
pigeonholes of what was deemed right and proper for their
stations, whether this did violence to their own natures and
growth needs or not.

Today, perhaps the most important freedom that is
emerging in the lives of transition people is the weakening
and blurring of rigid expectations of what a boy, girl, senior
citizen, worker, priest, and so on, should be and do. Not only
are the classic roles, such as male/female and parent/child,
blurring and broadening, but so are the multitude of other
roles that make up social life. The days when men can't weep,
women can't take the lead, children can't challenge, and
grownups can't caterwaul are coming to a close. What a piece
of freedom this is!

Previously, a person might have experienced life imprisonment in such role stereotypes. As these cages are now
opening, the fuller and more multidimensional human can
emerge, though perhaps stumbling and blinking against the
brighter light for a bit. Men and women can find their lives
enriched as they become more free to take up the skills, attitudes, or temperaments once confined to the opposite sex.
High school teachers, scientists, and even ministers are not
now so tied to the pillories of social righteousness. Children
are not automatically consigned to childishness, and adults
are not so stranded in "maturity".

In simply being our transition selves, we are breaking up
the more encrusted institutions of our society and forcing a
massive remodeling and expansion. For instance, the U.S.
Census Bureau has finally had to incorporate the category of
unmarried cohabiters into its statistical profiles.

As the social fabric loosens and the pace of change
quickens, we are also "unfrozen" by a marked increase in the

fluidity of institutions, relationships, and thought habits. Fewer situations or patterns now retain their forms long enough to solidify into rigidity. At the personal level, this means that we are all beginning to resemble migrant birds more than trees with deep taproots. Most of us are more on the move physically, interpersonally, and, most importantly, inside our heads. Fewer and fewer people now spend their entire lives in the same place, with the same family and friends, in the same career, and with the same views and feelings. This is an era of mobility; it would be hard to find anyone who now lives in a world that is the same as the world into which they were born. Examine your own life, and you will probably find this to be true.

Most prevailing theories of human nature were developed in more stable, slow-moving times, when people remained little changed throughout their lives. However, a growing body of recent evidence demonstrates that human beings become much more changeable when they live in ever-changing societies. Old notions that people are stamped for life by early psychosexual incidents or Pavlovian stimulus-response conditioning are being exploded and replaced with more holistic theories. Unfortunately, the old images still abound in behavioral science textbooks.

People's increased freedom to choose from a greater range of opportunities has been concretely documented. This freedom extends from decisions about the smallest things to major life choices. With each passing decade, fewer children follow in the occupational, religious, or residential footsteps of their parents. Mass-production technology and distribution have allowed the world's greatest books and music to become easily available to an ever-increasing proportion of the populace. In the old Western frontier of America, there were perhaps only half a dozen potential spouses within a day's ride; now the average person encounters hundreds of possible dates, lovers, and mates. Corner newsstands and tele-

vision programs display opinions that would formerly have
been suppressed as blasphemies. The unthinkable is now
being thought, and the unspeakable is being said in public.

However, we who are living through these transition times
know that things are not always as rosy as the last few para-
graphs suggest. For some readers, these comments will have
the hollow ring of any army recruitment poster. *But they do
show that we've gotten somewhere.*

Here's the down side of the loosening. As we are released
from old constraints and find more opportunities, we also
find ourselves adrift in more uncertainties. Our modern
human achievements are also the source of many of our agonies and unsettlements. It is no accident that the "age of individualism" is also the "age of anxiety." Nor is it coincidence
that both the promise of a technical wonderland and the
threat of world ecological catastrophe are in sight for the first
time in history.

We, the transition people, have what might be called
"position-anxiety": vague but persistent insecurity about our
place in the world. Who hasn't been plagued by this, at least
now and then? Yet who also hasn't asserted his or her rights as
free a human being to make independent choices of job,
friends, opinions, sexual behavior, religion, and so on?
Because we are more free to choose, we are also more anxious
about choosing. "Nobody tells me what to do" is a statement
with a poignant double meaning.

In the earlier historical spirals, people's positions were
mostly bestowed upon them; people knew their places. But in
our transition times, people arrive at their own places—which
are less and less determined by birth, sex, race, or nationality.
Consequently, people are anxious about their positions and
rather preoccupied with achieving and maintaining them.
Widespread in our times is an obsession to secure what Ernest
Hemingway called "a clean, well-lighted place"—coupled
with an insecurity about losing it. This position anxiety is fur-

ther compounded by the fading of clear expectations about what these achieved positions mean—hence all the books on such things as raising children, the woman's role today, how to succeed in business, and stress reduction.

It is ironic that we who have more power as mobile citizens and common stockholders in our societies are more plagued with anxieties than earlier humans who had less say in their own affairs but who were forcefully trained to be more accepting of their lots.

So, the loosening of the social fabric and social role stereotypes leaves us both freer and more adrift. What do transition people do with this deep dilemma?

People sometimes resolve these insecurities by giving away the freedoms they have. They give their country over to dictators; they opt for low-risk, low-reward careers; they semiconsciously tie themselves down with acceptable treadmills. They have the negative image of free time as a burden and of footlooseness as waywardness. From this perspective, freedom is chaos. These people are not yet *ready*. This response can be a backlash against the transition times, with people seeking refuge in the security of security. Sometimes this is simply based on the fact that they are scared. (And who isn't scared sometimes?)

There is a related response: resistance to the transition process. For the last two decades, men in barber shops have joked that "you can't tell the boys from the girls." Every recent social movement of note, such as the civil rights movement, the women's movement, and the human-potential movement, has spawned a condemning backlash. The rise of right-wing political conservatism and religious fundamentalism in our times is partly a concerted resistance to these transitions. Because change means the end of the old along with the birth of the new, there *is* usually some wistfulness involved in it, so this response is understandable. These reactionary responses usually involve attempts to hold onto facets of the spiral that are being transcended. They are dominated by old images and are forms of traditionalism.

What about tradition? Is it safe? Not really—not when it does not fit the realities of the times. For instance, traditional thinking about warfare in this day of the thermonuclear global village certainly is unsafe even for the traditions one might wish to preserve. A nuclear winter would ask no political questions.

How about the work ethic? Are idle hands the devil's workshop? American society is moving away from this mentality, but "wasting time" still creates guilt for many people. They feel bound to at least *appear busy* to others. Why? Because workaholics still engender admiration. Sometimes when I tell people I'm lazy, they look at me quizzically as if I have confessed a perversion.

Old images suggest that there may not be enough jobs in the new era. This is a fixed consideration again. Is there anyone to feed and educate and help? Is there anything to discover? Are there any lives or families or civilizations to create? Operating according to tradition and fixed considerations during rapidly changing times can get a person into a real stew.

How we define situations is often up to us. We can see flux and change as opportunity; we can see flexibility rather than instability; we can see the loosening of traditional ties as unfettering rather than dissolution and chaos.

There are many possible responses to our transition times, and most of us have used them all at some point, in some areas of our lives. Resistance is one such response. Another response is that of ritualism—an attempt to reduce insecurities about an unstructured changing world by scheduling existence into a series of rituals performed by certain rules. This, too, can be an escape from the uncertainties of more freedom. The rituals become an end in themselves, imposing a kind of artificial order on the universe. Often buried in this response is the hope that if the orderly rituals are carried out, every-thing will somehow be all right. When outside events inter-vene to upset the rituals, the participants usually become very distressed and may feel that their world has been shattered.

Participants in ritualistic responses, in attempts to over-come their feelings of vulnerability, often even ritualize their intimate relations with spouses, parents, and children, who will then often complain of emotional deprivation in the rela-tionships. The participants also tend to ritualize their reli-gious and spiritual lives. As realities change, all these rituals usually begin to feel increasingly hollow and superficial. When real events impinge, it is then a personal shock.

Another response to our times is that of alienation—a sour estrangement from one's circumstances and times that has received so much attention from social theorists, from Karl Marx to Sigmund Freud to people sitting in urban coffee houses. This response has often been romanticized in "seri-ous" modern art and literature, and it is the impulse behind the punk-rock movement. The alienation theme was expressed in the sixties by Bob Dylan's "Subterranean Home-sick Blues" ("twenty years of schoolin' and they put you on the day shift") and in the eighties by the bumper sticker that read "Life Sucks."

Alienation has some short-term psychological advan-tages. The alienated person's position is "invulnerable" because nothing matters; this is nihilism. The person is freed from conventional constraints, but there's no place to go. This position also justifies a "who cares" self-indulgent amorality. Ironically, however, it is hard to really enjoy the self-indulgence because of the generalized estrangement. This response tends to produce a descent into cynicism, pessimism, and negativity that is a self-constructed psychological and spiritual imprisonment.

Yet another response to our transition times is that of sim-ply enjoying the transitional circumstances to the best of one's

ability, combined with a vague hope that it will all come out
well somehow. The increased freedom from traditional constraints is celebrated as "party time." Youths frequently manifest this for awhile when they first move out from the family
nest. Ironically, their parents also sometimes manifest this
response when their child-rearing duties have lessened.

This "enjoyment" response can indeed be something of a
celebration of our milder, more open times. As individuals
find themselves freer than they have been (perhaps for many
lifetimes), there is an understandable tendency to cut loose a
bit, like kids turned loose in a candy store. After, perhaps,
centuries of struggling just to stay alive and find a bit of shelter from a stark environment, some people just want to be
comfortable and let it all hang out for awhile. This is understandable too.

This response may be a form of playful self-indulgence,
but it is often neither very permanent nor very harmful. Problems may arise, however, if the playfulness produces unpleasant
consequences. The pleasurable weekend fling may, for
instance, result in a pregnancy and the agonizing dilemma of
whether or not to get an abortion. Or one may become
addicted to recreational drugs. Or the bills may come due
after the credit card buying spree. Freedom can be intoxicat-
ing, but one can get in trouble while under the influence. A
heartening note is that I continually run into people who have
successfully survived such binges and come out on the other
side. I have come to personally suspect that the human spirit
eventually outgrows anything and everything.

Sometimes, in response to massive changes, people will
decide to die. When change "reshuffles the deck" of positions and opportunities, some individuals feel utterly bereft
and overwhelmed. If they do not find new lifestyles with new
rewarding games, statistics show that they move into a "high
risk category." That is, statistics demonstrate that these people
are likely to diminish, sicken, and die.

Dying is a way of aborting life-courses that people find untenable *from their viewpoint.* In Chelsea Quinn Yarbro's *Messages From Michael,* Michael points out that it is not the fittest who survive, as Darwin asserted, but the most flexible. In Jane Robert's *Seth Speaks,* the discarnate being Seth has suggested that "quality of life," which is a personal judgment call, is more basic to people continuing their incarnations than subsistence level alone. If you give people a strong enough reason to live (in their *own* eyes), they can recover from just about anything.

The above responses are "side trips," historically speaking, as we move through our transition times into the upcoming spiral. All of us engage in each of these responses at various times and in different areas of our lives. (For instance, we may ritualize our communications with co-workers or allow some aspect of our lives to die.) These responses can haunt the life experiences of individuals, but in the larger scheme of things, they are marginal to the evolutionary process. It is no accident at all that the words *transitional* and *transitory* (meaning "temporary" and "fleeting") have the same roots. Resistance, ritualism, alienation, playful self-indulgence, and even death are, it seems, only temporary pauses in the evolvement of our future lives. Maybe such side trips are always manifested during the transition periods between spirals. Things sometimes have to fall apart a bit before they can fall back together again at a higher level.

During transition periods, there is an almost inevitable polarization of the populace, a divisive allegiance to either the old world or the new, but not to both. As a recent example, during the eighties we simultaneously had the blossoming of the human potential movement and the ascendance of Reagan conservatism. History suggests that similar splits accompanied the earlier transitions but that the new evolutionary spiral always won out.

There are now a great many people who are actively reaching toward the future in their thoughts and dreams and activities. The basic tension between greater personal freedom and greater ambiguity seems to be a psychological and spiritual catalyst propelling large numbers of people forward into taking an active hand in *creating* the new spiral and breathing life into it. Maybe the side responses are like the caterpillar pausing before becoming a butterfly.

Once upon a time, when life was more stable and slow moving, contemplation of the future might have been a leisurely endeavor, done in the parlor or library over a snifter of brandy. Perhaps this was never really true, but it certainly is no longer true, for two big reasons:

1. The future is rushing upon us more rapidly than ever before.
2. We are awakening to the fact that we will come back to inhabit the world at a future time and directly, personally experience the situations we are now creating.

Chapter 5

HEALING
THE IMBALANCES

One quality of each new emergent historical spiral is that it heals or ameliorates some of the problems and inadequacies of the earlier spirals. The Agricultural Spiral provided more subsistence essentials than the previous ones. The Industrial Spiral extended material comforts and active participation in the society to much larger segments of the populace. And the emerging spiral is already providing humanity with a more flexible, user-friendly social fabric that has fewer constraints.

One characteristic of the last two spirals has been gross imbalances in some of the fundamental cosmic energy polarities. These imbalances have produced many of the ills we have experienced historically and are experiencing today. They are so deep-rooted that a great many people do not even see them as imbalances but accept them as part of "the way things are." However, as awareness rises, more and more people are beginning to clearly see these imbalances and the havoc they wreak. When they are perceived, it is shocking how insidious and pervasive they are. The good news is that they are beginning to be balanced and healed in our transition times. In part 2, I point out how these imbalances have deeply influenced many aspects of our lives, from environmental crises to how much money is in our pockets, to organized religion, to our private sexual experiences.

There are many fundamental polarities, and different mystical traditions present them with different imageries. The three basic ones haunting our modern civilization seem to be

1. male / female

2. materialism / spirituality

3. self-interest / collective-interest

There are a myriad of other polarities such as rationality / intuition, left-brain / right-brain, introversion / extroversion, inner-directed / other-directed, and we / they, but these seem to be either aspects or consequences of the more basic three.

Both individuals and societies can manifest these polarities in very unbalanced ways, in which one pole is preeminent over the other. Such preeminence of one pole is never total, for a complete absence of any pole is impossible. For example, if there were *no* spirituality, one couldn't be alive. If there were no awareness of others, one would be an utter autistic psychopath and wouldn't be able to survive. If one had no male energy, or no female energy, the resulting endocrine imbalance would probably kill one off at an early age. No pole is ever entirely absent—but it can certainly be way out of alignment. How these energy polarities and their imbalances operate will become clearer as each of them is examined more closely.

MALE / FEMALE

One of the most obvious imbalances in today's world is the ascendance of the masculine energy principle, yang, over the feminine energy principle, yin. In the famous Chinese ideograph of yin / yang (and in human sexual relationships) their ideal form is an endless intertwining covalence, but in our civilization their intermix has become extremely skewed, with the masculine pole ascendant and the feminine pole almost in shadow. Some writers have claimed that the ascendant masculine pole has led to the rapid human colonization of the planet and the swift rise of technology, although this is a *very* questionable assertion. Intuitive, gentler factors have retreated into the shadows and byways of human living in almost every sphere. We experience this lopsidedness—as both men and women—directly and continually; it is not just an abstract or mythological principle. It is, for example, no more abstract than one's next impoverished encounter with a member of the opposite sex. Male energies flood the auric fields of the planet like ghetto-blaster radios turned up too loud.

This polarity goes far beyond penises and vaginas. A handshake is masculine, a hug is feminine. Justice is masculine, compassion is feminine. A warrior is masculine, an artist is feminine. However, a too-masculine warrior is crude and brutal, while a too-feminine artist is ineffectual.

A single pole, when exaggerated and without the ameliorating, balancing influence of its other pole, *is always destructive.* With the male principle dominant, people speak of the *conquest* of nature, of *taming* the wilderness, of going to the top, of subduing and controlling. It is probably no accident at all that a giant intercontinental missile, preparing to launch, unmistakably resembles an erect penis. As another example, people say that one candidate or sports team *beats* another and that afterward the team members *score* with the girls. In his *blitzkrieg* agendas, Hitler spoke incessantly of forcing another country to her knees. You can supply your own interpretation of this image.

Three of the major world religions—Christianity, Islam, and Judaism—have traditionally supported and strongly encouraged dominance of the male principle. The Koran states, "Men are in charge of women. Hence good women are obedient." The Bible is filled with male chauvinist passages such as "A man is the image and glory of God, but woman is

the glory of man!" (1 Cor. 11: 7-9) or "Wives be subject to
your husbands as to the Lord. For the husband is the head of
the wife as Christ is the head of the church" (Eph. 5: 22-24).
Male Orthodox Jews include the following words in daily
prayer: "Blessed art thou, O Lord our God, King of the Universe, that I was not born a woman." Historically, the major
religions have also excluded women from the clergy. Their
position is "auxiliary."

This orthodox religious bias is not just something that
used to be. During the last month, while I was idly spinning
the television dial, I twice heard television preachers quote
these same biblical passages and admonish their listeners to
live by them. These are "rearguard actions."

Maybe the exaggerated male energy was necessary to carry
us through the stark conditions of earlier historical spirals.
This claim has been made by some (male) philosophers, such
as Freud and Darwin, although I think it is very questionable.
We might now be inhabiting a kinder, gentler world if the
exaggeration had not occurred. Today, however, this imbalance has become life threatening. With modern people's
rising awareness and expectations of greater personal freedom, it is becoming more and more unacceptable.

In our transition times, there is a rise of feminine energy
throughout the world. The women's movement is but one
visible indicator of this. The loosening of traditions from
earlier spirals is freeing people from personal imprisonment
within one gender pole or another; men are freer to weep and
women are freer to be successful outside the home. The percentage of women in what were formerly men-only occupations such as law, medicine, and business is still small, but it
has been steadily increasing for the last three decades. For
example, the proportion of those receiving medical degrees
who are women has risen from less than one-tenth in 1972 to
around one-fourth in 1990. In the same period, the proportion of those receiving law degrees who are women has gone

from one-fourteenth to almost one-third. The barriers are coming down. Massive statistical evidence, such as increasing female enrollment in advanced professional schools, suggests that this trend will continue in our future lives.

However, as one of my editors, Barbara Hand Clow, has pointed out, rebalancing requires more than women becoming manlike, since this by itself only compounds the imbalance. What is needed is the rise of feminine energies in both men and women and within our social order. For instance, doctors need to do more nursing, and scientists need to be more intuitive. Men caring for infants and children is an example of this type of shift.

Imbalances are not just abstract points. You can see them in the streets of our cities and hear about them in our counseling rooms. They distort relationships, culture, and the experience of living, so they are worth our attention.

The poles of a given polarity are not competitive with each other in any sense; this notion is itself an aberration born of the distortions caused by the imbalances. Therefore, healing the imbalances does not in any way involve a pendulum swing to an ascendance of the other pole. Nor are the poles "opposite" except in our own distorted imaging. The phrase "opposite sex," for instance, displays how deep-seated the gender imbalance has been. The "battle of the sexes" is a war of attrition with no winners.

Instead, balancing involves integration of the poles. However, integration is not a pallid, lackluster canceling-out of the virulent energies of either pole. It is a transcendent fusion, a blending in which, together and combined, the poles are much more than each could ever be alone. The left hand and right hand together can do far more than either can do alone.

Each pole, when integrated and balanced, enhances the other. There is then a continual two-way flow between the poles. Imblances block this two-way flow and cause innumerable social and individual maladies such as various widespread bodily ills and psychological disturbances, ranging from frigidity and impotence to family violence, assault, and rape. Conversely, as the poles become integrated, individuals become empowered and released from long-standing travails. *Imbalances are crippling.*

MATERIALISM / SPIRITUALITY

The imbalance between materialism and spirituality has been talked about for many centuries, but nothing much has come of all this talk until recent years. Those people heavily enmeshed in material games and goals have paid some homage to those people sequestered in spiritual paths, but in many ways the two poles have simply gone their separate ways. In the past, men of the world pursued worldly matters and pious men pursued other-worldly concerns. During the last several centuries, women were mostly domesticated creatures, "tamed" and cared for like pet animals. There were, of course, exceptional women of influence like Queen Elizabeth, but they were exceptions and often manifested male energies. Some native cultures have been nonsexist, matriarchal, and spiritual, although these have had little influence on Western civilization.

Worldly concerns were clearly ascendant over spiritual ones, although sometimes they were given a spiritual nod, like a sprig of parsley adorning a luncheon plate. Despite the rhetoric, however, there was actually little real dialogue between the two poles. There were a few exceptions, such as the Quaker philosophy that strove to integrate the two poles, but the point is they also *were* exceptions. There were also underground traditions in the West, and isolated coteries in the East, but these *were* underground and isolated, apart from the main historical stage of expansion, colonization, and industrialization on a planetary scope. It is only in our own time that some of these more spiritually balanced traditions have come into mainstream world awareness.

By itself, the materialistic or mundane pole strands people at a coarse vibration level. And by itself, the spiritual pole is ineffectual, at least on the physical plane. The mundane pole has clearly dominated, at least during the Industrial Spiral, which is now ending. Some writers have argued that the materialistic pole dominance, like the ascendancy of masculine energies, was necessary to accomplish the human infestation of the world and the triumphs of technology. This argument is questionable because we are now coming to realize that all things flow directly or indirectly from the spirit.

Additionally, the materialistic dominance has become hazardous in our times and has led to impoverished lives. Materialism alone manifests as a lack of "spirit" that is necessary for any real sense of aliveness of experience; its followers dwell in a two-dimensional *flatland.* On the other hand, accentuation of spirituality alone can produce a sense of dwelling in a no-man's-land, of inhabiting neither this world nor the next. Blockage of the flows and interchanges between these two poles can also produce innumerable psychosomatic ills, as medical science is now documenting. When there is low spiritual awareness, people are also vulnerable to religious demagoguery and doctrinal manipulations. Hell, although a human invention, may become more real to those who are spiritually bereft than their own spiritual essences are, making them vulnerable to psychic browbeating and blackmail.

With materialism ascendant, and the flow between it and spirituality partially blocked, people have become stranded on the physical plane with no "communication from home." Mundane predominance has also allowed levels of uncaring ruthlessness (as in war and other violence) to occur that would not happen if the material and spiritual poles were more in tune and integrated. The callousness toward our fellow humans and other life-forms, so widespread throughout our recent history, arises from this imbalance.

Such imbalances are not user-friendly. They rob us of many things, including close affinity with other beings—one of the most valuable things in the universe. They create schisms wherein we each live only half a life.

When stuck manifesting only one pole, people often *can't control themselves;* their behavior is unbalanced. Rampant, overwhelming compulsions, obsessions, and physical addictions are some of the results. Greed, sexual fixations, and crime are others. Psychiatrists have developed elaborate nomenclatures for these various undesirable states but have usually missed the underlying source as being these imbalances. Therefore, much of their theorizing has turned out to be rather useless and has in fact sometimes *reflected* the imbalances. For example, a great deal of psychoanalysis is sexist and attempts to explain away spiritual experience as hallucinatory.

Part of the materialism / spirituality imbalance has been the exaltation of rationality and logic over intuition and emotion. Rationality alone builds a flat world, a linear social landscape devoid of warm colors and currents, a world of wristwatches and appointment books where even friendship and lovemaking are matters of punctuality and efficiency. Generations of people are trained to inhabit this landscape of straight lines and standard operating procedures. But despite the training, something ancient and soulful within us says, "No."

In *Choosing a Path,* Sri Swami Rama has put the question of the rational mind very well. He says, "If someone wants to become a murderer the mind will help him and if he wants to become a sage the mind will also help him."

In our transition times, many writers have documented the growing revitalization of spirituality and the beginning of its integration with the mundane. The results of this beginning integration are fantastic. Illnesses that have resisted all conventional (mundane) medical treatments are abating, multitudes of lives are being enriched, and our societies are becoming more multidimensional.

One area where the healing of this imbalance can be seen is the dawning reintegration of science with mysticism. Formerly, when a physicist demonstrated an experiment, the audience would nod cogently, but when a yogi demonstrated arcane abilities, the audience would dismiss them or look for the trick behind them. Today, Nobel Prize–winning scientists are sounding more and more like Buddhist masters, and mystics are starting to use the scientific method to demonstrate empirical evidence for their assertions. This rapprochement can also be seen in the works of bestselling science fiction writers such as Robert A. Heinlein, Marion Zimmer Bradley, C. J. Cherryh, Arthur C. Clarke, Roger Zelazny, and a host of newer authors. It is also evident in the *Star Wars* and *Star Trek* films.

SELF-INTEREST / COLLECTIVE-INTEREST

The third basic polarity that has dogged the events of the last historical spiral is that of individualism and communalism. Whether we are happy about it or not, most of us are keenly aware of ourselves as individual units, but are far less aware of ourselves as part of a living whole. We have split the cosmos into "I" and everything that lies outside of "I." Our imbalanced awareness of "I" therefore immediately *strands us in separateness,* within which we weep over lack of intimacy and togetherness.

There has been a rampant "psychological bias" in Western civilization during recent times, in which the individual has been exalted at the expense of a sense of community or communion with all other things. Even if "you" and "I" succeed in forming a bond of commonality, our position then usually becomes that of "we," separate from "all the rest of them." This creates contentious gangs at the neighborhood level and contentious countries at the international level. The fact of our worldwide interconnectedness has grown faster than our awareness of it.

We have also created an imbalance, related to this polarity, between competitiveness and cooperation, in which competitiveness has been exalted. For example, in a series of small group experiments, social psychologist Harold Kelley and his associates found that men considered the cooperation mode of interaction weak and passive. Like the other imbalances, this one also runs so deeply that it is hard to see it for the distortion that it actually is. The competitive urge has even been promoted as a "law of nature," but scientists now tell us that conflict is far rarer in nature than we have been led to believe. Cooperation, symbiosis, and accommodation are actually the most common practices in nature—and in successful human interactions.

Many non-optimum things flow from this individualistic imbalance. On the world stage there is extreme rapacious capitalism, which has produced the reaction of extreme rapacious communism, both of which are nuts and neither of which has worked very well for the populaces involved. This imbalance has led to exploitations on all levels and has increased individual and collective karmic burdens.

The niches in which we individually dwell have expanded until they have each taken in the entire planet. Our daily lives and our eventual destinies have become inextricably intertwined with more and more of the formerly distant aspects of the total world environment. This great interdependence ranges from the air we breathe and the food we buy to the incomes we make, the kind of education we get, the safety of the cars we drive, and the airplanes we ride in, to the summons to arms we may receive in the mail. So stark individualism has become simply unrealistic. Self-centered people cannot resolve our difficulties, let alone uplift humanity. Both the mystics and the recent Nobel Prize–winning scientists tell us that there is really no such thing as a solitary act.

The predominance of individualism suppresses awareness of our underlying planetary interdependencies. In many ways we all sink or swim together, and because of this, stark individualism is self-defeating even in the not-so-long run. In our transition times, there is growing awareness of this fact of life.

When the polarities are out of balance and one set of poles predominates, the subordinate poles are usually repressed and pushed to the sides of society. Those who are stuck in an exaggerated manifestation of one pole will often derogate and engage in belittlement, contempt, and name-calling toward the other. Those who strongly manifest the subordinate poles may be accorded nodding recognition, but they are almost always regarded as impractical, naive, and not fully competent in handling world affairs. Women were denied the right to vote, the clergy were relegated to a Sunday-morning time slot, and those concerned with our collective planetary fate were shunted to the fringes of society.

Happily, all of this is changing. Each imbalance is also an evolutionary force propelling us forward and impelling us to grow. As we grow in awareness, we are finding that either pole of a given polarity alone is somewhat sterile, like half a song. We can use our increased consciousness of these polarities to determine what is still aberrant in human society.

The three polarities discussed here form an interconnected bundle that includes other polarities such as the left-brain/right-brain polarity. With balancing and centering, each pole can be raised to new heights of intensity, direct experience, and enjoyment. Each pole intensifies as the pair it belongs to comes into balance. The resulting qualitative change in the experience of living is likely to be a major foundation for the upcoming spiral. The wholeness this will create can result in a different kind of human being who can create a different kind of world.

Chapter 6

AWARENESS
RISING

As the visionary physicist Peter Russell and so many others have pointed out, each new evolutionary stage is an emergent new reality, qualitatively different from the preceding steps.

Just as we cannot live in the past while we are in a changing world, so also we cannot anticipate or lay careful left-brain plans against the future—because the future won't be just an extension of the present. In twenty years, many of us will be working at jobs not yet invented or named; we'll be using products that now exist only in some bright child's imagination. Who among us can say what will be the economics or living arrangements or headlines or morals of that future day?

Yet all around us are signs of this new era. We can see the markers of the deeper historical tides in the same way we can determine the passage of a rocket by its contrail. One of the most important of these markers is the significant rise in individual and collective awareness and expectations around the world. This has many individual and collective implications. Rising awareness and rising expectations are propelling us into the new historical spiral. The grassroots force of this has often taken leaders and commentators by surprise, as, for example, in the ground swell national hue and cry over environmental crises and widespread corporate crimes.

At first glance, the claim that awareness is rising might seem startling, if not untrue. But take a closer look. Child abuse and wife abuse may actually be greatly *declining* in our times. Our *rising awareness and collective rejection* of them are producing media stories and legal actions, but these may not accurately reflect the rate or percentage of these occurrences. Roman parents and medieval Japanese husbands were never called before the courts for the way they treated their spouses or offspring. There is even the biblical injunction that prevailed for many centuries: "Spare the rod and spoil the child." In former times, family violence was just a part of life; today we are outraged by it.

Rising awareness and expectations are demonstrated by the many ways in which individuals and groups are more easily *outraged* today than ever before. World opinion is now dismayed at apartheid, but during the nineteenth century entire American Indian populations were moved about for the convenience of settlers and placed on reservations, where they had fewer rights than South African blacks. Often throughout history serfs have been bound to land they farmed for the nobility landowner; this practice was accepted by priests and philosophers alike. "Darktowns," where American blacks were confined and segregated, were a fixture of the American South for decades. In the Middle Ages, there was the Children's Crusade to free the Holy Land, in which hordes of children marched off, mostly to die or be sold into slavery by other Christians. Today these kinds of practices are becoming more and more unthinkable—which steadily reduces their likelihood of happening. Intergroup atrocities have occurred and are occurring in our time, but what is *new* is that people the world over are increasingly shocked and dismayed by them.

A modern example is the subject of marital rape. Until recently this concept was regarded as a contradiction in terms because women were morally and even legally expected to be sexually dutiful to their husbands. A famous quip on this subject cost a California politician his career. He said, "If you can't rape your wife, who can you rape?" This statement was nothing new. What was new was the massive public outcry over the statement.

A different, very powerful way in which rising awareness and expectations are propelling us forward is through a comparative sense of *relative dissatisfaction or relative deprivation*. Absolute conditions do not matter as much as people's assessment of these conditions compared with how they subjectively feel the conditions *should* be. For instance, a woman in a Third World country might have formerly compared her lot with that of her mother and felt content or resigned. Now she might compare her lot with that of women in industrialized countries and feel far more dissatisfied and motivated to change things. Probably unknowingly, she has become a force impelling us all toward the upcoming spiral. She wants more freedom and equality and material comfort, and she will be broadcasting these urges both physically and psychically. She will be an active agent, with others, for changing the vibrational field of her locale, which will therefore never be the same as it once was.

This example, multiplied millions of times, has given rise to a pervasive collective urge and striving throughout the world for "a better life." The force of these strivings should not be underestimated. Conservative attempts on the part of privileged groups to keep and enhance what they already have at the expense of the rest of the planet and population are only temporary, transitory impediments to this force, like a weak dam across a swollen river. *Rising awareness and expectations cannot, in the long run, be denied.*

Concomitant with this force is an *enlargement* of worldview. Worldwide mass communications are eroding localism and provincialism. Distant parts of the world have become real places to hundreds of millions of people through video film footage. More and more people are physically *seeing* more of the world than ever before. The mass media, for all its many distortions, is slowly educating the entire world about the undeniable facts of our increasingly interdependent lives. Most forms of isolationism are becoming simply ludicrous and untenable, as even the rabid despots are finally learning. Local dictators are slowly discovering that they can't afford to be isolated from worldwide goings-on.

Increasing awareness is therefore a collective matter as well as an individual one. Just as there are shifts in individual awareness levels, so there are collective shifts reflected in such things as popularity ratings, public opinion, the standard operating procedures of institutions and agencies, and the overall climate of opinion within a society (or town or family). Things that a populace will accept, put up with, laugh at, and not stand for are important "atmospheric conditions" influencing what happens in a society. These comprise the mass thoughtforms through which society and its members assign meanings to the objects and events in the world. What is so important is that these awareness changes reverberate on all physical and vibrational levels. As these change, the culture's worldview evolves. For instance, the eminent public opinion analyst Daniel Yankelovich found that in 1950, 80 percent of those questioned in a national poll felt there was something wrong with people who preferred to remain single, but that by the 1970s this proportion had shrunk to 25 percent. He also found that the percentage of those who automatically trusted the federal government to do the right thing shrank from 55 percent in 1958 to 28 percent in 1978. Such major shifts in mass thoughtforms influence all levels of a society. Populations are beginning to become more watchful. There is probably no country left on Earth today where something like the Roman gladiatoral arena would be tolerated. Nor would the Hindu custom of *sutti*, in which a widow was expected to throw herself into the blazing funeral pyre of her dead husband, be acceptable in any modernized country. We've made some progress.

If the society as a whole becomes more enlightened, it becomes easier for the individuals living in it to evolve. The evolvement of the individuals then feeds back into the society to increase the collective awareness level. This process can be self-feeding and self-perpetuating.

Growth in collective awareness levels is sometimes hard for us to see because we are living through it. But this growth can be glimpsed in silhouette by noticing the changes in what we laugh about and what we question. When the somber morality plays of one generation become the successful farces of the next, it is apparent that something significant is happening to the collective psyche. If we can joke about our leaders, our sexuality, our illnesses, and our religions, we aren't so bad off.

As awareness rises, the general level of tolerance also increases. There is voluminous documentation to show how this increased tolerance has been occurring. As one example, in 1924 the pioneer sociologists Robert and Helen Lynd found that 94 percent of the high school students in a midwestern U.S. city thought that Christianity was the one true religion and that all peoples should be converted to it. In 1979, in a follow-up study, sociologists Theodore Caplow and Howard Bahr studied the same midwestern city and found that the proportion of students holding this rigid sectarian viewpoint had shrunk to 38 percent.

At low levels of collective awareness, many cruelties occur that would not happen at higher levels. Sleepwalking political candidates would have little support at higher collective awareness levels. Fewer people would allow others to live in anguish. Large numbers of people would not be left uncared for. Technological abuses, environmental atrocities, and commercial frauds would become too unpopular to flourish. The coarser vibration pools and locales would begin to dissipate like predawn mist. *These things are already happening* as planetary awareness and expectations are rising. Few of us would now accept or sit still for the brutalities that were commonplace events of even half a century ago. This fact alone is a virtual guarantee that our future lives will be gentler than our past ones have been.

The rising of the collective awareness of humanity obviously has a long way yet to go. Also, there is rampant factionalism between those at different levels of awakening. For example, environmental problems have become a very real concern for many people, while others don't know what the concerned people are talking about and are contemptuous. Those concerned with overpopulation clash with those who assert, "Be fruitful and multiply." Those seeking inner spirituality are condemned as blasphemers by those dependent upon external dogmas.

The more aware people don't always win in the short run. This was the case with the recent surge toward democratization in China. These factional conflicts often accompany the transition periods between spirals, but however convulsive the transitions, the new spiral prevails.

At the turn of the century, the visionary psychologist William James wrote that compared with what we ought to be, we are only half awake. The Russian mystic P.D. Ouspensky wrote in the 1940s that to "awaken" for man means to be "dehypnotized." More recently, New Age therapist Chris Griscom wrote in *Ecstasy Is a New Frequency*, "Each one of us must awaken and know that we are our own teachers, that we are our own healers, that we are our own priests."

Increasing awareness brings such knowledge back home to people. As evolution continues, this seems to happen naturally, like children coming into puberty or the leaves opening in springtime.

How far can our collective worldwide awareness and expectations rise? Who knows? Let's see.

Chapter 7

THE
DARK SIDE

If there has been one miscalculation common to most visionaries, prophets, and "Aquarian Conspirators" since the dawn of history, it has been the underestimation of the stubborn inertia and malign defensiveness of the status quo. Perhaps it is well that the visionaries have made this miscalculation—if they hadn't, they might have despaired, and humanity might have been robbed of much uplifting through the centuries.

Individual "transformers" will often set themselves up for frustration and disillusionment when they underestimate the inertia and tenacity of the status quo barriers and the old mass images buried within them. These barriers resemble thick glacial ice as it melts in the light of an Alaskan landscape.

Those seeking transformation sometimes prematurely celebrate the new birth. Enthusiastic readers of Marilyn Ferguson's *Aquarian Conspiracy*, a fine and landmark book, might have been shocked and dismayed by the ascendance of the Reagan/Bush power bloc in the United States and some of the retrogressions and backlashes surrounding it. With new visions in one's mind and heart, one can easily become an impatient gardener who misses the rhythm of the seasons and growth. But even as one despairs, the blooms arrive.

One would have to be naive indeed to say that there is no

dark side to our transition times. The signs of turmoil and lurking potential unpleasantries are too obvious to ignore. Gloom-and-doom prophets of all persuasions and backgrounds have examined our situation and asserted that things cannot continue as they are—that our present course will sooner or later lead us inevitably to one kind of disaster or another. They are absolutely right, but...

Humanity's *present course,* if we were to continue on it, is an inevitable road to catastrophe. However, the crucial point is that the deepest historical tides of change, acting as evolutionary drivers, are so strong that *it is impossible for us to stay on our present course.* We *can't* remain as we are. It is true that many people may be dragged kicking and screaming into the upcoming historical spiral, but things have never remained on the same course for very long in human history. It is *how* they will change that is our primary concern.

The problems of our transition times are like "labor pains" in the birthing of the new era. Each of the areas discussed in the next section of this book has its pressing problems, and these problems have both personal and sociological implications. Also, they seem to alter even as we try to grasp and understand them because of the underlying historical tides of change.

It is not helpful to be too coolly intellectual about these situations, because they can produce real tragedies in the lives of individuals. I know that there are some readers who have recently experienced personal tragedies or who have the threat of tragedy looming in their lives. I do not make light of their situations because I've been there—we've all been there. I'm only saying that if we step back and look, there are some good reasons to smile.

There is evil in the world, and we've all given and received some of it in past and current lifetimes. Echoes and resonances of all the past historical spirals are with us in memory, and these echoes exist in our institutions and cultural patterns.

Some of this historical residue is far from pleasant, as the swelling legion of past-life regression therapists can attest. However, we are on a progressive journey up and out of this residue, and I'll bet you a nickel we make it!

There is a wonderful quotation from Richard Bach's *Illusions:* "What the caterpillar calls the end of the world, the master calls a butterfly."

There are a few broad factors that tend to prolong both the prevalence of current forms and the heritage of forms from earlier historical spirals. These factors act as impeding barriers to a smooth transition into the upcoming spiral. If we understand these barriers, we can help dissolve or circumvent them. Many people are currently manifesting one or more of these barriers in their thoughts, feelings, and actions, but this does not necessarily make them bad people; it is just where they currently are. Undue antagonism toward them would probably only entrench them further in their positions. Cordial dialogue is more productive. Beneath any differences, all people are evolutionary companions on the road.

Here are some of the important barriers to our transition into the new spiral:

KNOWLEDGE GAPS

Most of the world's population was socialized and educated to live in times that are already gone. The information and strategies that may have been correct for the 1930s, the 1950s, or the early 1970s are already outmoded to some degree. Many of us are in the peculiar situation of living in a new world, while our heads are still partly in the old one. The facts of investing, international affairs, sexual relationships, child raising, and so on, are just not the same as they were even a couple of decades ago. The current realities of our world are different from what many people learned when they were growing up. For instance, even three decades ago there was some stigma attached to needing to borrow money; today it is part of our way of life from the level of the individual to the level of the government. As two other examples, savings accounts are no longer very good investments, and the wedding night is almost never the first intimate unveiling.

Subliminal resonances from previous lifetimes also contribute to people being out of tune with modern times. These resonances can cause people to embody past positions, fears, and compulsions that can mislead them badly, as many human-potential writers have pointed out. As an extreme example, cavalry-charge thinking in a nuclear global village is unrealistic, to say the least. So is fear of starving to death when you have a good job and hundreds of pounds of food in the house. (How many diets has this dread interfered with?)

There are also the knowledge gaps between new discoveries made by experts and the wide dissemination of these discoveries throughout the populace and into the heads of decision makers. This is often a problem even between researchers and practitioners within a given profession, let alone between that profession and the wider public. For example, this rift between researchers and practitioners has often happened in the medical profession, despite its very extensive internal communication networks. As another example, textbooks in many professions seem to be perennially a step or two (or ten) behind the times.

Knowledge about the holographic nature of our universe, about the Greenhouse Effect, pollution, or the immunological system of the body, may lurk for years, even decades, within the leading edges of discovery without becoming widely known. There are looming societal problems, such as water-table pollution and the loss of domestic markets to foreign competition, that knowledgeable experts desperately attempt to teach the public and the decision makers about, with only slow and uncertain success.

For all these problems, however, we are still in better shape with respect to the knowledge-gap barrier than we've ever been. Technology has given us massive communication networks and information systems unlike anything that has existed before, and these systems get better year by year. The knowledge gaps don't last as long as they did in previous historical spirals. In previous spirals, it might have taken months or even years for most of the world to become aware of an event; now it takes only minutes. So the human race's collective "reaction time" has speeded up tremendously.

Lack of knowledge means ignorance, and ignorance goes hand in hand with naiveté about what we are doing. In the midst of massive changes, our past knowledge and experience are still useful, but they cannot serve as a clear guide. Continual change makes us, who are involved in it, continually innocent.

Until very recently, Western civilizations have held something of a mystique about innocence—it was exalted as an archetypal state of purity and grace. In terms of Western religious heritage, loss of innocence has been viewed as a "fall" from clean to dirty, from pure to tainted. The role of "angel" was foisted upon children and virgins, and the rest of us were expected to feel vaguely guilty. Some fathers still feel that when their daughters have become sexually active they have lost their "purity." One certainly wouldn't want a "pure and innocent" airline pilot or dentist!

Innocence can mean ignorance, about everything from intimate personal matters to the arena of international affairs. When people are ignorant, they can't be very self-determined or free, because freedom requires knowledge of the environmental field and the competence to cope within it. The ignorant tend to be simply used—by others, by social institutions, and by history.

In our own time, ignorance is simply an individual and collective threat. In our ignorance, we hurt one another, walk away from our opportunities, and befoul our living space. We *must* grow wiser and not leave our destinies in the hands of hucksters and hooligans.

NORMS AND VALUES

Most people live by the morals and standards of the tribes into which they have been socialized. Even when they bend or break the rules, they still usually hold these rules as sacred ideals. The fact that an anthropologist might call such rules "local customs" is lost on those who are embracing them and living (or dying) by them. The cultural roots of people can be identified by the norms and values they manifest. These give people symbols to live by and yardsticks to measure themselves and others against. However, there is no guarantee whatsoever that cultural rules are rational or beneficent or "user-friendly" to humans. These rules may circumscribe and constrain. Embedded within them can be such things as the imbalances examined earlier. As times change, these cultural standards may become more and more out of sync with current realities. For example, very high birth rates, through which one proved one's manliness or womanliness by producing many children, made good sense in times of high death rates, but they make less and less sense in modern urban environments with very low death rates and problems with overpopulation. As another example, the norm of "counting coup" among the Plains Indians, in which a young brave proved his manliness by dashing forward to touch his enemy, may have worked just fine—until he faced the U.S. cavalry. Then its practice became deadly and suicidal.

Since norms and values are seldom the same from one society to another, it should not be surprising that different historical spirals are characterized by different sets of prevailing morals and standards. People are usually rather fervent and emotional about the standards they hold dear, so they also usually condemn and belittle those who don't share these standards. This makes compassion toward others (let alone love) *very* conditional. This is why there is widespread indifference toward homosexuals who have contracted AIDS: "Well, they deserved it" is the response of many people on the streets and from some television evangelists. During the transition times into a new spiral, some people who strongly embrace the prevailing standards also likewise condemn those on the leading edges who are experimenting with alternatives and prototypes of new forms. Many solid citizens feel that unconventional scientists, fervent environmentalists, and spiritual visionaries are somehow *disreputable.*

People can also manifest morals and standards that are echoes from lifetimes in previous epochs. These are almost guaranteed to be out of step with current times. Manifesting such echoes, men may find themselves being physically aggressive toward opponents, and women may passively wait for men to make the moves. Other people may subliminally "worship the sun."

The upcoming historical spiral shows every sign of being a more enlightened one, so we can expect its norms and standards to be more enlightened. As the visionary priest Matthew Fox suggests, we may, for instance, embrace a religious value of "original blessing" instead of our current one of "original sin." Also, we may come to perceive the feminine aspects of godliness, with its "womanspirit" archetype.

One of the most important aspects of raised consciousness is the ability of people to see and evaluate the morals and standards by which they have been living and judging others. When people can evaluate their standards, they can then begin to change them in the direction of more universalism and compassion. As the pioneer New Ager Ken Keyes, Jr., is fond of saying, it is far nicer to be loved than to be right.

FIXED IDEAS

Fixed ideas are buried within the prevailing belief structures of every society or group within a given time period.

These ideas can consist of virtually anything, they are thoroughly learned by the society's members, and they generate their own self-fulfilling realities. When an individual holds fixed ideas, he or she is considered rigid; when a society holds fixed ideas that we share, we say, "That's the way things are." As Seth, channeled by Jane Roberts, has exhaustively depicted, these fixed considerations lock a person or society into a very limited perspective about human nature and multidimensional realities, keeping the person or society tuned to one television channel, so to speak. Such ideas are not only limiting, they may also be flatly erroneous from a cosmic perspective. "The white man's burden," "the divine emperor," "decent women," and "bad girls" are expressions that may seem archaic, even amusing to us now, but people have often lived and died by them. Thomas Kuhn, in *The Structure of Scientific Revolutions*, and many subsequent researchers have documented how even scientists, for all their public relations about open mindedness, get stuck in fixed ideas and are often highly prejudiced against their replacement. In physics, there is the tyranny of Newton's mechanistic theories, which have crept in and colored the theories of almost all other sciences, including mainline psychology and conventional medicine. (What a loveless, lightless worldview!) These ideas are buried within the very languages with which we learn and think. Based on these ideas, we try to confine others to the ways that we ourselves are confined. Fixed ideas are like steel rods in the mind.

When we have fixed ideas, everything beyond them seems *unthinkable.* Then when the unthinkable occurs—as it so frequently does in history—the individual or organization or entire society carrying the fixed ideas may fall apart. Our problems may actually be simpler than we think. Perhaps it is our fixed considerations and rigid mass thoughtforms that are obtuse.

There are two things that strongly act to hold fixed ideas

in place: low awareness levels and isolation from competing alternative ideas. This is why religions, nationalistic dictators, and cults often employ practices that insulate their followers from alternative viewpoints. They want their followers to hold the "proper fixed ideas."

However, the various facets of modernization act to reduce the influence of both these factors—by creating a general rise in awareness and by eroding provincialism. The "window on the world" aspect of mass education is especially potent in this regard, as will be discussed in part 2.

VESTED INTERESTS

This barrier rests upon the predominance of individual self-interests over collective-interests. In one way or another, it manifests as the gaining and maintenance of personal privilege at the expense of the larger good. It is usually whitewashed with various justifications, even religious sanctions, such as "the righteous will prosper," but in reality it is a win-lose situation that eventually becomes a lose-lose one for all concerned. Vested interests operate strongly to maintain the status quo, that is, things as they are. This of course acts as a brake against the unfolding of a new historical spiral or much progress of any kind, for that matter. It also makes the ride through the transition times bumpier than it otherwise would be. The staggering military budgets that have drained the economy of the United States and made it the world's largest debtor nation are, for instance, in good part the result of vested interests on the part of the Pentagon, the giant defense contractors, and state governments eager to bring monies into their areas. The fact that the United States has about twice the number of elective surgeries but a shorter life expectancy than England is in part the result of vested interests operating in the American medical establishment. The continuing male domination in a great many areas of life is partly due to the concerted maintenance of vested interests. The stubborn, cov-

ert resistance to sane ecological policies results from the
entrenched vested interests of large corporations.

Pursuit of vested interests can get very crazy, as it often has
in previous history. Many bloody revolutions could probably
have been prevented if the vested interest groups of their
times had made some concessions. If these interests had
accommodated, even partially, to the demands and desires of
the rest of the populace, they could have probably kept much
of their privilege—and their heads.

From a spiritual perspective, and from what we now know
about the Beyond, the single-minded pursuit of vested interests is sadly amusing. It is certainly worthwhile to be successful on the physical plane, but to be obsessed with securing
and maintaining an advantaged position is to be obsessed
with the most transitory sorts of things. We cannot take the
positions and privileges with us at the end of our incarnations,
but we do take the coarse-vibration-level experiences, prejudices, and blocked energies with us as unwelcome baggage.
This does not condemn us—nothing does—but, ironically, it
puts us in *poor* positions in the Big Game of spiritual growth
by giving us more to work through and transcend. The
spiritually evolved are much more able to cope, protect themselves, and enjoy the experiences of Earth living than those
who wholeheartedly amass physical-plane wealth and power.
The latter strategy turns out to be misguided and self-
defeating.

If individual vested interests are self-defeating, the opposite exaggeration, in which individuals are sacrificed for
groups, is also utterly unworkable. To the best of my knowledge, every attempted communist regime has had to become
a police state in order to even continue existing. These
regimes have also failed to decently feed and house their own
people, and their tyranny over individual lives is unmatched
in history. In recent years, many communist countries such as
Russia, Vietnam, and Poland have themselves admitted that

their systems haven't worked, and they are now seeking to change their ways. It seems a good bet that neither unbridled capitalism nor extreme communism will be part of the upcoming historical spiral because both have failed to work.

FUTURE SHOCK

Who hasn't felt a bit tremulous their first day on a new job or on a first date? These are small examples of what Alvin Toffler called "future shock" or "the shock of the new." Many studies have shown that when people are faced with new and unexpected circumstances they often go into states of upset, disbelief, and numbness. Perhaps a snake feels this way just before it sloughes off its old skin in springtime.

When conditions change, we are faced with something new and unknown; the more extensively and rapidly the conditions change, the more this is true. If we have our lives somewhat organized, the changes make us feel disorganized, even when we see the changes as positive. If we are not sure whether the changes are good or bad, we are likely to feel anxiety as well. If we disapprove of the changes (because of fixed ideas, norms and values, or vested interests), additional negative emotions such as fear and resentment may be heaped on top of the other emotions. Those experiencing future shock can become very uncomfortable within themselves, and they can make others uncomfortable by their resistive manifestations.

People experiencing future shock are very resistive to transitions and new spirals. They may feel that everything is slipping away—that their familiar world is fading before their very eyes. This reminds me of a time when I sat one night at dinner with an elderly man and woman who eloquently lamented the fact that the America they had known was gone.

In our transition times, future shock manifests as an overwhelm by aspects of modernity and a numb retreat from them. Women's liberation, unisex, computers, the international arena, the new music, science fiction, the New Age movement, and space exploration, may all be wondrous to some, but to others they may seem bewildering, threatening, disreputable, and somehow blasphemous. People experiencing future shock often have a rosy, distorted nostalgia for the past, and if they are active, they may support ultra-conservative and backlash movements or causes. This barrier has always been operative in history and, as long as times keep changing, we can expect it to continue to operate.

When one encounters future shock in others, it seems best to meet them with open dialogue and understanding rather than with putdowns and antagonism, because these latter positions only entrench the people further and help "prove" the correctness of their trepidations. Dialogue and understanding don't always work, but at least they don't add gasoline to the fire. Also, I have seen many people come through future shock of one kind or another with flying spirits.

If the other barriers are not too heavily involved, future shock can be merely a temporary process for "getting used to" changes. When people are given a little space and time to do so, their resistance fades and they adjust to the new situations. I recently heard a seventy-year-old woman defend the right of young people to experiment sexually, asserting that the world had changed and that you couldn't judge people by the way things used to be.

All of these barriers can be interlocking and mutually reinforcing; they can interweave like patches of tough crab grass that stubbornly resist removal. As much as anything else, they may determine how rough the transition to our future lives will be. They are not always detrimental, because sometimes they act as needed brakes on runaway trends. They are part of the human story; we have all no doubt been on both sides of these barriers at various times. From a higher perspective, they almost seem like the trembling pause before a metamorphosis.

The interweaving of these barriers is exemplified by our current environmental situation. There is an extensive knowledge lag in this area; many people don't know about our massive tainting of the planet's ecology, or, if they have heard about it, they don't really believe it. Traditional Western norms and values mandate that humanity should endlessly exploit the environment, with few if any repercussions. Vested interests carry on fervent fights in the courts and in Congress to do what they want, and they usually win. A great many people react with numb, future-shock disbelief over the raw facts of acid rain, the warming Greenhouse Effect, a potential nuclear winter, deteriorated air quality, and water-table pollution. Meanwhile, more and more humans walk around with persistent coughs and watering eyes.

However, even on the subject of the environment, which will probably encompass our major social problems of the upcoming decades, there is good news. Amidst all the bad news, the good news is that national polls in all Western countries show a rapidly increasing collective concern with environmental issues. Also, the governments of these countries are taking tentative first steps toward *doing something* about these issues.

These barriers are almost an intrinsic part of physical-plane living; they have historically been with us through our individual and collective journeys, although how fiercely and cruelly they have manifested has varied tremendously. In our modern times, there seems to be a meltdown of the harsher expressions of them. We should not expect them to disappear as long as humans are evolving on this planet and as long as we are still learning the lessons of physical life. However, as the gross imbalances that feed them come into better alignment, we can expect their manifestations to gentle. In our future lives we will still be running into people exhibiting fixed ideas, vested interests, and knowledge gaps, but if they do so with fewer dark emotions, our social and psychic environ-

ments will be much more comfortable, and it will be far easier
to "negotiate settlements." In fact, there is now a fast-
growing new profession called "conflict resolution" that
applies the principles of "Game Theory" to negotiating win-
win solutions for disputes arising over these kinds of barriers.
It is being employed in situations ranging from hassles
between neighbors to international affairs.

NEGATIVITY

There is yet another factor interfering with smooth evolvement that is the most basic and insidious barrier of all. It has
been called "evil," "the forces of darkness," "the work of the
devil," and so on, but none of these capture its essential
nature.

This factor alone creates the vast majority of the pain and
unhappiness and fear we encounter on the physical plane. Its
forms of expression are multitudinous, ranging from jokes at
another's expense and verbal criticisms to "mind fucking"
and the atrocities we are treated to in the daily newspapers.
We practice it upon ourselves and upon one another in ten
thousand and one subtle and direct forms, and we seldom
realize the costs. It is the major contributor to our failures, our
illnesses, our stress, and our accidents. It gives us what Seth
calls our "negative meditations"—our continuous brooding
over our situations and prospects. It dampens our enthusiasms, sours our successes, and interdicts our pleasures. It
makes us timid and cautious. And it is to some degree self-
perpetuating because of our belief in the "eye for an eye" philosophy.

This might seem like an overstatement about the role of
negativity in human affairs, but I invite you to examine the
last time you were upset or hurt and to look for the part that
negativity of some sort played in the incident. Try to locate
the sources of the negativity—there may be several. Also, see
if the negativity was something you "passed on" to others, at

least by being dour and irritable.

When I was in high school, there was a mean game going around called "Pass It On." You would come up to someone, hit or squeeze their arm painfully, and say, "Pass it on." The outcome was a contagion of bruises. Since that time I have seen a great many people, under a wide variety of circumstances, play similar games at the personal, social, and spiritual levels.

Negativity can perhaps be best understood as *pollution* of human space. This pollution is even more pervasive than chemical toxins, because it can add its drab coloration to any and every human endeavor. In fact, there is every reason to believe that our outer environmental pollutions are a reflection, directly and indirectly, of our inner emotional pollutions. For example, as we manifest the imbalances discussed earlier, the resulting actions add pollution to the biosphere.

We rightly worry about the effects of smoking on nonsmokers. The effects of negativity on others are far more dangerous. Even those striving to rise above negativity can be easily reinfected by its vibrations, as any seeker can attest to. Some people are so entrenched in negativity that they will attack others for being positive. There is also a psychic leakage of negativity—telegraphed from one person to another—a process not unlike giving each other the flu.

Negativity explains why positive affirmations and creative visualizations don't seem to work for some people. I have known people who have experimented with these techniques and have not been able to make them work. Later, in conversation, I found that their deeper, stronger beliefs were that such things really didn't work and were hopeless. Their positive visualization was therefore weak, while their negative imaging was stronger and deeper. (Surprisingly, the positive visualization sometimes worked even under *these* conditions.) Unfortunately, negative imaging also works.

We cannot really dodge the negative images and energies

that form part of the holographic Earth energy fields and some portions of the lower astral plane levels. They are, it seems, part of our collective human heritage and must be lifted and released bit by bit. A great many people of good heart have helped alleviate this collective burden by practicing the power of positive thinking, feeling, and acting throughout history. If they had not done so, the race would have drowned in darkness long ago. Also, there has always been much of the world and our experiences in it that has been positive, from great moments to simple pleasures. Throughout our evolvement we have been accompanied by a symphony of small pleasantries that have made life worth living. These are always there, but we must look at the dark side as well, in order to grasp our transition times and what they might become.

The real news is that in our transition times a growing number of people are working to release and erase negativities from their lives and their environment. Successful techniques for doing this are now becoming widely available and known—more than ever in history. For instance, such books as Louise Hay's *You Can Heal Your Life* and Shakti Gawain's *Creative Visualization* are selling hundreds of thousands of copies.

Fortunately for all of us, positive energies telegraph too. Most of us do many things that enhance the lives of others. There are a lot of people currently in the world who are busy helping others improve their lives and their spirits. As one example, sociologist Dr. Lois Lee has had an 80 percent success rate in helping runaway children escape prostitution by helping them establish positive lifestyles. Sociologist Rosabeth Kanter has, as a consultant, successfully humanized many bureaucracies by demonstrating to corporations that a more user-friendly workplace increases profits. On a more directly spiritual level, New Age counselor Kathleen Vande Kieft summed up this positive energy nicely in *Innersource:* "Soon your inner transformation becomes reflected in everything that surrounds you."

There are currently a great many elements striving to rise above the negativities in our collective consciousness. Such an uplifting would, all by itself, guarantee a brave new historical spiral.

Part Two
OUR ONCE AND FUTURE LIVES

History is a journey every one of you is making.
MICHAEL / CHELSEA QUINN YARBRO

We should not expect people "on the path" to behave as if they had reached the goal.
PETER RUSSELL

Ultimately, souls start out on earth in the denser energies and work their way up into the higher and finer energies.
ORIN / SANAYA ROMAN

Is it possible that the whole history of the world has been misunderstood? Yes, it is possible.
RAINER MARIA RILKE

Chapter 8

TECHNOLOGY

Technology has received heaps of praise for enriching and saving human lives, and it has received a lot of condemnation for its ravaging of the environment and its threat to planetary life. Those who condemn technology do so while sitting within its comforts; those who praise and enjoy technology often inadvertently add to its destructive consequences. Technology has always been vitally important in human life. Throughout our evolution, our level of technology has been the underpinning for what kind of lives we have lived.

Our technology, as we fumble with it, has given us such grave problems as ecological pollution, ozone-layer depletion, urban blight, and nightmarish weaponry. However, we cannot abandon it and return to some more pristine era. Even if it were possible to do so, such a move would create unimaginable anguish and suffering for billions of people. It would involve all of us doing without glasses, books, air conditioning, telephones, and electricity. (This could be likened to an extended version of what happens during an electrical power failure.) Without mechanized agriculture, at least half of the world's current population would quickly starve to death. We can't go back, but we must become more aware of what we are doing, technologically.

With each ascending historical spiral, our technological ability to intervene with the environment and to shape it to human desires has dramatically increased. At the same time, our use of technology during each spiral has reflected whatever imbalances have existed within that spiral. The technological developments of one spiral have provided the necessary platform for the developments of the following spirals. Our current lifestyles rest directly upon all the technological developments of the earlier spirals. However, because of technology's ever-increasing effectiveness, abuses of technology are becoming ever more dangerous to us.

The development of primitive tools went hand in hand with the Hunting and Gathering Spiral. A few technical refinements led to the Gardening and Herding Spiral. Irrigation, the plow, and better weapons supported the development of the Agricultural Spiral. The Industrial Spiral came into being and flourished as a result of a host of technical inventions in the fields of tool making, transportation, and communication. Technology also has a major hand in the birthing of the new, as yet unnamed spiral that is beginning to emerge. Whatever happens, dark or light, our future lives will owe much to technology.

Each succeeding spiral has also made it possible for more souls to be incarnated on the Earth plane. As we move into space, there is no theoretical limit to the number of bodies available for spirits to dwell within. So, in part, we may also owe our next bodies to technology.

Science fiction writers have usually described our future lives in the context of future technical wonders. They have intuitively sensed technology's crucial role. However, they have also usually embodied our present gross imbalances in their descriptions: masculine energy dominance, materialism, gross competitiveness, and violence. The result is that many science fiction tales are merely Westerns or 007 stories transplanted into space. Most of them have simply projected our present spiral into a technological future of interstellar ships, magical gadgets, and glittering weaponry. However, without a massive shift in our collective consciousness level, the likelihood is strong that we would destroy ourselves before we reach the stars. Almost none of these writers have taken a rise in planetary consciousness into account in their scenarios, so their visions embody our present distortions and negativities. However, consciousness is never the same from one spiral to the next, so the future will be a surprise to most of these writers, too.

We can too easily get lost in the details of the many controversies surrounding technology. What we need are some of the bottom lines. There appear to be four main ones.

First, technology is now *potentially* able to satisfy all of our basic human survival needs on a mass basis. The fact that it has not done so everywhere only reflects our transitional imbalances and tribalisms. With each passing year, we become more able to feed, house, and care for more people with less effort and potentially less destructive side effects. The development of automation, robotics, fish farming, solar energy, and biotechnology strongly suggests that there is no end to these trends in sight. As the brilliant, innovative psychologist A.H. Maslow pointed out, when basic needs are satisfied, individuals can go on to pursue social and spiritual interests. It only remains for us to bring these technological potentials into full manifestation.

Second, modern computers, telecommunication systems, and massive data-storage-and-retrieval systems have made it possible for the current Information Society phase of the late Industrial Spiral to arise and flourish. These things have led to a qualitatively new and different information and communications scene. We are still discovering what all this might mean. However, this Information Society is not the new spiral; it seems to be the last, transitional phase of the Industrial Spiral that has prevailed for several centuries.

Within our current lifetimes, our information (data) bases have increased a thousandfold. Our archives are now bulging with more data than we currently know how to handle. This data includes everything from half a century of national public opinion polls to world information on hundreds of different societies, to trillions of bits of new data on the solar system, to a century of relatively precise weather data, to the tracking of a half century of economic investment performances. Computer networks make most of this data available on a mass basis. By hooking up a personal computer to a telephone line and paying modest fees, one can access many thousands of times more information than was available in the Alexandria library.

Given this situation, many new things are possible. For one thing, we can now monitor regional, national, and world trends and theoretically take measures to soften or prevent such things as economic depressions and disease epidemics. We are beginning to discover "safe" and "unsafe" geographic locales, based on differing death and illness rates. The promise here is intervention before catastrophe, but better links between data researchers and decision makers must be developed for these potentials to be fully utilized. This massive data base has, for instance, shown us the Greenhouse Effect (a world warming trend) while we are still able to do something about it, but we have not yet taken most of the actions necessary to resolve this problem.

Massive data bases also make possible what is called "secondary analysis," the researching of bodies of accumulated data. One can, for instance, do a study of all the accumulated specific research ever recorded on the effects of loneliness on health. (This data shows that loneliness is a major health hazard.) Or one can do a comparative study of the role of women in over 350 different cultures investigated in the last century by anthropologists. (This data documents the pervasiveness of the male / female imbalance.) Such secondary analyses are producing information (and sometimes wisdom) at an unprecedented rate.

These secondary analyses are also producing a healthy infusion of truth into the physical plane. They are blowing away rhetoric, anecdotal assertions, and many of the grand armchair theories of yesteryear. This is often becoming troublesome for politicians and others asserting fixed considerations. For example, we can document beyond argument that women are underpaid in the workplace relative to men and underrepresented politically at all government levels. Such data also drives holes through the sweeping assertions of Freud, Darwin, Marx, and other theorists who manifested part of our non-optimum mass thoughtforms. (The subconscious is not a cesspool of lustful antisocial slime, humans are not just "thinking animals," ferocious class struggles are not the major propellant of history.) Finally, the mushrooming databases are bringing to light the distortions introduced by generations of zealous humans into the major religions of the world.

The third technological bottom line for us is the movement of humanity into space. In this area, the science fiction writers shine in their predictions about what these developments might mean materialistically. Space scientists and sci-fi authors read one another's works continually, and many people have dual careers as both.

Before long now, humans will be living in space on a permanent basis, becoming less and less dependent on Mother Earth, like children who have grown up and left the nest. Space colonies mining the moon, beaming unlimited energy to Earth, and building additional new space colonies are all now almost within our grasp. These advances are bound to cause major shifts in perspective for humanity. After this progress, the technological developments become somewhat more inconceivable. But then, any modern hardware store or supermarket would be totally inconceivable to a dweller back in the

Agricultural Spiral. This is "the high frontier." What all we will find out in space escapes our grasp now, but it certainly will not be the same old thing. However, if we do not handle our imbalances along the way, we will just end up exploiting space as we have done with our native planet.

Perhaps the most startling idea about space technology is that once we move into outer space our available resources become, for all intents and purposes, inexhaustible. We are so deeply programmed with the idea of scarcity and the necessity of struggling and competing for everything from food and shelter to creative jobs and pretty bodies that untold abundances are hard to imagine. These untold abundances would be not just for the "winners" but for every human being as birthrights. The technologies that would allow tens of billions of humans to live lives far better than today's "lifestyles of the rich and famous," within our solar system alone, are already on the drawing boards.

Does this seem farfetched? Well, it is farfetched. But remember, the common facts of life within any one spiral are always utterly farfetched to those dwelling in previous spirals!

The fourth technological bottom line is the marriage of science and mysticism. Here, too, there are so many developments unfolding worldwide that no single person can begin to keep track of them. For example, technologies for consciousness raising are proliferating, being refined, and being disseminated on a mass basis. A number of "mind machines" are available to help to synchronize the left and right hemispheres of the brain, and there are yet more startling developments. The human aura is being photographed, and its changes under stress, disease, and love are being tracked. New, highly refined scientific studies of extrasensory perception are being carried out. Out-of-body experiments are being conducted. Near-death mystical experiences are being rigorously documented and their life-transforming after-effects are being explored. Groups are working to empirically map the astral planes.

The future implications of these developments are simply profound and awe inspiring. *We are fast approaching a point of incontrovertible, scientific, empirical proof of the spiritual essence of the human being, of life after bodily death, and of reincarnation.* (In truth, we have already reached this point, but there are still many barriers to full acceptance of the documentation and proof.) The scientist and the mystic are rapidly becoming the same person.

As one of near-death researcher Kenneth Ring's respondents said, we're going to have to rewrite all the textbooks. These emerging findings will necessitate a fundamental shift in perspective on the part of the peoples of Earth. Resistance on the part of fundamentalist-religion adherents will be very strong, as will the resistance of those with a deep materialistic perspective, but the direction of changes in popular thinking about death, karma, human nature, and the living cosmos are now unmistakable and irreversible.

There are, of course, many problems surrounding technology and our use and abuse of it. In our zeal and greed, we usually rush to apply it before we have fully mastered it or explored its implications. Then we sulk because it doesn't work out as we had hoped or because it carries a price we hadn't counted on. Often when we introduce a new technology, it has unintended consequences that create new problems even as old ones are eased. Social theorist Alvin Weinberg has called this the "technological fix." One example is pesticides, which give us more food but pollute our air and water and the very food they give us. Another example is the drastic reduction of the infant mortality rate in a country, which then gives the country the new problem of masses of half-starving children. Our technologies have also become so good that we can now commit "ecocide"—the destruction of the Earth's biosphere—for the first time in history. And we could do this in a dozen different ways.

There is no doubt that our glittering array of technologies also has some side effects of which we as yet have no inkling. What are the consequences of decades-long use of aluminum-based deodorants? Does continuous exposure to microwaves from myriad sources have any long-term effects on health? Very few of our certified medicines or chemicals have been tested through the entire life cycle of human beings. As with asbestos and radon, we often learn about side effects and long-term consequences of technology the hard way, to our sorrow.

These are real problems and sometimes real tragedies, but in a broad sense the entire evolutionary spiral has been a long sequence of "technological fixes," each round of developments impelling and triggering the next round. As we move into space, our interfacing with technology becomes even more delicate because our environment is becoming even more of an entirely human construct. Therefore, we must become more environmentally aware, and we must become more skillful and responsible in the art of living in friendly symbiosis with our environment.

The up side of technology is that with each successive spiral we have become more able individually and collectively to manufacture our environment from whatever raw materials are available. There is no end in sight to this trend. Increased control of our environment frees us increasingly from impediments and constraints such as space, time, and natural conditions. We can more and more bend conditions to our desires and imaginings, and this liberating process is only just beginning. What these desires and imaginings are or will be rests, of course, with us.

Chapter 9

WORLD
METROPOLIS

One of the most visible and obvious results of evolving technology has been the massive rise of cities. Through the historical spirals, there has been a progression of constructed habitats from furnished cave to village to town to city to metropolis to world megalopolis. This has been one of humanity's primary collective physical-plane transformations. The whole world is now going urban—physically, psychologically, and socially.

Urbanization on a massive world scale has been one of the most important events of the twentieth century. Why? Because it induces a basic shift in how people live, feel, and think. The urbanization of the world is a primary vehicle carrying us from traditional societies into the now-emerging world community. It is also a main part of the process for loosening traditional bonds and increasing freedoms that was examined in part 1. And it is the necessary foundation for the rise of a true world culture, which is now beginning to occur.

Statistics show us how this urbanization has been occurring, over time. For example, as late as 1790, the time of the first United States census, only one out of twenty Americans lived in (small) cities. By 1860, the figure had risen to one out of three, and by the mid-1970s it had risen to three out of four. Data gathered by the United Nations shows similar trends for other countries of the world.

We also know from worldwide statistical data that industrialization and urbanization go hand in hand. As one example, Albania, which is just beginning to fully industrialize, is only 34 percent urban, while West Germany, one of the most industrialized nations in the world, is 95 percent urban. Also, the influence of cities is increasingly reaching into the remaining hinterlands to further erode the tribalism and provincialism still existing there. Urban television, magazines, newspapers, and books go almost everywhere now. You can now live a very urban life in the country.

Behind these bare facts is the fascinating story of the city and its role in the evolvement of humanity. The historical development of cities is closely intertwined with the unfolding of the evolutionary spirals. There were no cities in the Hunting and Gathering or Gardening and Herding spirals because the existing rudimentary technology could not support them. Cities first arose during the Agricultural Spiral, although they were very small compared with those that exist today. For instance, it is estimated that Athens had perhaps only thirty thousand citizens and an equal number of slaves during its heyday. Typically, preindustrial cities contained no more than five thousand to ten thousand inhabitants. Even large regional centers of power such as Troy and Babylon were almost always under forty thousand people. Due to transportation systems that were slow and could carry only small loads, the surrounding countryside could feed no more.

The majority of preindustrial cities were dirty, dark, disease-ridden, and dangerous. People seldom went out at night except in groups or accompanied by armed guards. Everyone carried weapons. There were no sidewalks, no street lights, no sewage or garbage systems, no purified drinking water. The cities stank and were polluted beyond belief. Death rates were a third or more higher than in nearby rural areas, and, in fact, most cities maintained their size only through streams of new arrivals. Plagues were common occurrences. For instance, a plague in the early fourteenth century killed an estimated one-third of the people in London. Soon thereafter, a fire burned 80 percent of the city down.

If these conditions prevailed, why did anyone willingly live in these cities? Why were streams of newcomers attracted to cities each year from rural areas? For one thing, there was the promise of economic opportunities. Cities were the centers for trade and craftmanship and venture schemes. People also went to the cities for adventure and excitement—for a more interesting and stimulating life than the rural areas offered. New ideas, new art forms, new inventions, and new mysticisms have always arisen in cities. They were natural places for seekers of all kinds to go. Many people also went to the cities in pursuit of what the rural folk called "vice." Runaway sons and daughters, the dispossessed, exiles, and outlaws also found security in the anonymity of cities. People could escape from their pasts and start afresh by going to the city, and they could outrun bad reputations by going on to another. For all these reasons, and in spite of their dangers, cities appeared to many to be a desirable alternative to a life of the dull toil of farming, fishing, or foresting. All these reasons still hold true today and continue drawing people to modern cities.

Preindustrial cities were centers of commerce, specialized crafts and professions, the arts, religion, and government. They were also centers of excitement and "sin." In cities, things have always gone on, such as drug use, prostitution, and speculative blasphemy, that simply weren't allowed in the rural areas. In cities, entrenched traditions were questioned and heresies were concocted. Cities have always been somewhat disreputable in the eyes of the countryside dwellers that the cities ruled, administered, serviced—and exploited.

As the Industrial Spiral began, cities grew rapidly as

whole families moved to them in large numbers because of job opportunities. Industrial technology was applied to agriculture, which enabled the surrounding rural areas to feed larger and larger populations within the cities. Work hours per cultivated acre shrank to less than one-twentieth of what they had been previously, and yields per acre tripled. An average farmer could therefore produce sixty times more than before mechanization. This is an example of a very important trend that has continued throughout the evolution of the spirals, which is that a smaller and smaller fraction of the population is able to provide all the basic human necessities, such as food, for everyone.

As the decades passed, cities started to become cleaner and safer. Gas street lamps appeared in the early nineteenth century, and rudimentary sewage and purified water services began to be introduced. There was some fire and police protection. However, cities were still dominated by living quarters without separate bathrooms, where people sweltered in the summer and shivered all winter.

The average working conditions, which included a six-day, sixty-hour work week with almost no fringe benefits, would simply be unacceptable in the industrialized countries of today. Over the years, often in hard-fought and bitter struggles, workers gained concession after concession in working conditions, wages, work safety, vacations, pensions, and health care. Freedoms, benefits, and leisure-time increased until the very quality of life was transformed for the vast majority of working people. The proportion of the populace in the middle class swelled dramatically. Never before had these things occurred. As people poured into the cities and new cities sprang up all over the world, the collective profile of humanity was transformed. The cities themselves continued to become more and more interconnected with one another. Today, the planet's surface has become interlaced with an entire gridwork of cities, to the point where this network is becoming a unified metropolitan configuration.

Aspects of this transformation have been partly described, partly moralized about, by a long list of well-known social theorists including Karl Marx, Sigmund Freud, Emile Durkheim, and Max Weber. Since their theories partly reflected biases from earlier historical stages, their views about urbanization and modernization were somewhat negative. Happily, much recent research has proven their forebodings wrong. For instance, it turns out that most people do retain close interpersonal ties even in the heart of a city. These theorists mostly missed the postive characteristics of urbanization such as increased personal independence and opportunities.

The modern metropolis simultaneously epitomizes the greatest accomplishments and the gravest inadequacies of current Western civilization. Both factors reflect humanity's incredible collective efforts to master and shape the environment rather than merely exist within it. However, because of our major imbalances, this drive for mastery has often been extremely callous and environmentally unfriendly. Cities can so easily become asphalt jungles where blue skies and greenery are conspicuously absent.

Cities have retained something of a bad reputation because they have been judged in comparison to lingering rural-biased paradigms. Most appraisals of cities have been one-sided enumerations of what is lost when people move from small, sleepy communities to concrete jungles of noise and strangers. These portrayals grant that there is adventure waiting in the city, but this is often seen as the adventure of Orpheus descending into hell. A happy ending in such depictions is the hero or heroine emerging unscathed, having learned a lesson about the importance of traditional morality. In this peculiar situation, urban dwellers retain an anti-urban bias in their images.

Why is there a lingering anti-urban bias in the minds and

hearts of so many people? Even among the people flocking to
the new world metropolis? The answer probably lies in the
free-floating insecurity and anxiety of our transition times,
coupled with the fact that humanity is still learning how to
live a planetary urban life. When insecure or in doubt, people
tend to fall back on the images and attitudes of earlier spirals.

Urbanism's true faults come from humanity's relative
innocence about how to live in these new constructions. *Never
before in history have we had an urban populace.* Never
before has an urban lifestyle been the predominant mode of
human existence. Never before have cities stretched over
entire geographic areas and incorporated ten million people
or more. The negative aspects of city life may be "only" the
temporary mistakes and growing pains of our historical trial-
and-error learning process in which we know not yet what
we're doing.

An obvious challenge facing humanity in the upcoming
decades is to create cities that are both user-friendly to the
humans living in them and user-friendly to the environments
upon which they rest. We have made some progress in these
areas—cities are not quite the death traps they once were.
However, cities currently manifest extreme population densi-
ties and are the major sources of planetary pollution. *This is a
qualitatively new way of life with which we are still fumbling.*

Urbanism is so important because it is releasing us from
the bonds of earlier tribalism and traditionalism. We have
already come so far in this process that it is extremely difficult
for most of us to even imagine what it would be like to live
closely intertwined with only the same few dozen people all of
our lives. Most of us would find this to be a psychological and
spiritual straitjacket.

Urbanization has released individuals from the sometimes warm, but usually constraining, ties of close-knit kinship living and group identification. Urban dwellers must
fumble and grow, and make it or fail, more or less on their

own devices. *Our urban problems are the problems of greater freedom.* City builders had little or no inkling of the forces they were setting in motion. We were a species released before we were very well equipped to handle our release—or fully reap its promise.

The city is now humanity's earthly address, and that's not so bad. For instance, it seems strange to realize that, in terms of absolute resources and lifespans, even the ghetto dwellers in modern industrial nations are often better off than their forebears with respect to freedoms and opportunities. Even the gateless poor among us have more, and are less locked into physical and psychological ruts, than most of the nameless and numberless masses of previous historical spirals. Needless to say, this in no way justifies tolerating their abject conditions.

Perhaps the truly revolutionary thing about urbanization is that it is releasing the dreams and aspirations of people. It unleashes their hopes and fancies. This in turn produces restless and impatient people who are aspiring and seeking. They see that they are freer and more adrift, and they see the incompleteness of their emancipation.

Ironically, urbanization helps provide avenues of resolution for the very restlessness, impatience, and higher aspirations it has helped create. While releasing people into more freedom, it also provides a greater proliferation of alternative opportunities than ever before has existed. There is diversity available almost beyond belief in the urban setting. Check the *Yellow Pages* of even a small modern city—with a population of, say, fifty thousand—and you will find a veritable wonderland of specialized services, associations, training programs, clubs, and so on. Nose around a little and you will find many more that *aren't* listed in the *Yellow Pages.* And if you can't find what you're looking for, try the city down the road.

Cities certainly have a down side, particularly during our transition times. In cities there are concentrations of society's underclass and concentrations of hopeless substance abusers. Cities are also homelands for large numbers of those who are alienated and adrift. Also, for many, the new urban lifestyle means the down side of anonymity: loneliness. The "personal" ads in urban newspapers have, between the lines, a heartrending, desperate quality to them that almost makes you want to comfort the next person you see. Of course, the majority of the lonely are not even up to advertising. However, these things are not specifically problems of the city; they are problems of humanity. I have the feeling that, in the upcoming spiral, we will have life squads instead of death squads.

In developing Third World countries, these shifts from tribe to metropolis are taking place within a generation or two rather than over several centuries as they did in industrial nations. The result is socially convulsive, and their urban problems are magnified many times. However, they have an "urban field" to move into that already industrialized nations did not, and they have the chance to learn from the other nations' slower histories.

Almost all the work being done toward manifesting a new historical spiral is being done in an urban setting. Urbanism has gone far beyond a merely physical fact to become a dominant way of life.

As a new era approaches, we can see the beginning outlines of a world metropolis. The city is our new home and our ticket to further freedoms and opportunities and adventures. Using the best of technology, it is possible to leave the smog and the ghettos behind and, instead, bring in the trees and flowers and clear running water. The cities of tomorrow are as unguessable in their collective form and spirit as Los Angeles would be to an ancient Athenian.

Chapter 10

SOCIAL
CLASS

If somehow all class distinctions in the world were abolished and everyone were given an equal hundred thousand dollars, within ten years there would probably be just another class structure. However, it would be far more fluid, and have fewer entrenched and inherited distinctions, than any class structure currently existing in the world. The new system would be more "open," so that more people could move around from class to class, than in any system now existing. There would, however, be "the winners" busily trying to figure out how to protect and maintain their more favorable positions and pass them on to their children. Wouldn't you?

All known societies have had some sort of social class system. Nowhere on the planet are all the members of a population of any society equal to each other either in position or opportunity. Social stratification is a fact of human life on the physical plane. However, these class systems vary in their "fairness" tremendously. They have also varied throughout the earlier historical spirals. In the Hunting and Gathering Spiral there was not enough abundance to create very much class distinction, although the best hunters, healers, and craftspersons were a bit better off and had a larger portion of what little there was. In the Herding and Gardening Spiral more of a true class structure arose, usually based on ownership and heredity.

The Agricultural Spiral produced far more surplus and abundance. During its epochs, extremely rigid class structures arose, in which the class a person was born into was a predetermining factor in the life they subsequently lived. "A place for everyone and everyone in their place" was the slogan of this spiral. Class position was almost entirely hereditary, and the gap between the top and bottom of the class ladder would be almost inconceivable to us today. A tiny fraction of the population might own three-fourths or more of the entire wealth and land of the country, while most of the underclasses might be legally bonded to these owners. The privilege level of the privileged classes was something that people of no modernized nation would put up with. For example, a nobleman could usually beat a servant to death with impunity. Various forms of slavery and perpetual serfdom were virtually universal, and social mobility was almost nonexistent. Average life expectancy of the lower classes is estimated to have been less than half that of the privileged groups. (Similar conditions still prevail today in a few preindustrial areas of the globe.) We've come a long way since then, and no doubt many of us have had a hand in this coming.

During the early Industrial Spiral and the flourishing commercial era that accompanied it, the fossilized class structures began to break up—although not without some convulsive reshufflings and civil wars. Merchants, townspeople, independent tradesmen, and shop owners began to acquire more wealth and power and to challenge the old order with its entrenched inherited privileges. New frontiers opened up and traditions lost power—a trend that has continued ever since. It was a time when one could gamble one's life and win a lot or lose it all.

Today there are still class structures everywhere in the world, including all the "classless" communist societies. However, there are *crucial* differences between these modern class structures and the class systems of previous spirals. Two of these differences are especially important for our transition times and our future lives.

The first crucial difference is that a person's class position has become less a matter of heredity and more a matter of one's own achievement. It certainly helps to be born into a wealthy and well-connected family, but this is no longer the all-encompassing, life-determining factor it once was. Through education or entrepreneurship, there is far more potential upward mobility available to everyone, including women and minorities, than ever before. This looks like it will be a continuing and increasing wave of the future. It is still quite difficult to make it all the way from the bottom to the top of the social and economic ladder, but millions upon millions of people have moved up and out of poverty into more abundant lifestyles. Although the conditions of the poor in modernized societies still cannot be sanctioned, most poor people have far more than poor people had a century ago, so even the poor have advanced in life conditions and life chances. They also have more opportunities for self-realization than has any previous underclass. We could, of course, enrich the entire human race by substantially increasing their opportunities.

The second crucial difference from earlier class systems, and another optimistic trend, is the lessening of the gaps between the various strata of modern class systems. One example of this is the swelling of the size of the middle class in modern societies during the last century (a phenomenon mostly missed by the Marxists). There is also less of a total gap in wealth and opportunity between the top one-fifth and the bottom one-fifth of most modern populations. They are still a long way apart, but they used to be worlds apart. For example, in most industrialized countries someone in the top fifth makes about six times as much as someone in the bottom fifth, while in many of the Agricultural Spiral societies someone in the top strata would have made *thousands of times* more than someone at the bottom. In fact, during the later phases of the current Industrial Spiral, the whole collective class structure has risen. That is, the majority of people have risen in class position. Perhaps one-sixth of our populace is now below the poverty line, whereas in earlier spirals the figure might have been two-thirds or more. This is a great human accomplishment, whatever the remaining inequalities.

Some people feel it is a bit un-American to mention class systems because America has an ideal of being a land of equal opportunity. However, class position makes a real difference in people's lives. The higher the class position, the more a person is insulated from the environment and its impacts. A teenage child of an extremely wealthy family lives in a different world from a child of a successful professional, or one of a working-class family, or one of homeless parents, even though they may share the same geographic locale. Having several hundred dollars worth of car trouble is one thing for a wealthy debutante, another thing for a middle-class mother, and quite another thing for a lower-class welfare recipient. The car's breakdown is incidental to the upper-class woman, an inconvenience to the middle-class woman, and a desperate disaster to the lower-class woman. This is just an example of why the rising of the entire class structure is so important to our future lives. When the entire class structure rises, so that each person's resources and opportunities increase, everyone wins.

This is an important lesson. We can change our own class position, but we can also upgrade the entire class web—a game everybody wins, because people can then expand their focus beyond scrabbling for necessities.

Social researchers have done a great many studies of social class over the last few decades. They have found that virtually *everything* varies by class position, from health level to television-program preference to educational level to style of lovemaking to political and religious convictions. They have found almost nothing that is not correlated with social class, at least to some degree. Class differences were often so great in the previous historical spirals that the different classes spoke dialects that were mutually incomprehensible.

Aside from today's greatly increased fluidity within class systems and the lessening of the gap between class strata, there is another entirely different thing happening in our transition times: the driving importance of social class in people's lives is fading. Not so long ago, class position, and the raising and display of it, was a major preoccupation in the majority of people's lives. Now, more and more individuals are becoming concerned with other life goals such as self-realization, a designer lifestyle, or just enjoying themselves. "Keeping up with the Joneses" has become more of an outdated joke than a grim fact of life. With increased abundance and the rise of alternative goals such as those supported by the human potential movement, the importance of the class system is attenuating. Nowadays, people rarely ask about one's family background. More frequently one is judged, and judges oneself, as an individual, not just as an appendage of a family or other status configuration. At least in the rich, modernized nations, we are beginning to break away from our preoccupation with the class system and go on to other things.

Also, rapid social change continues to "reshuffle the deck" of class positions. Hence, one might personally experience being in several different class positions within a single lifetime. Of course, since people are more on their own, these movements can be down as well as up—but they are less fixed than ever in history.

Nations, as well as individuals, can be divided into classes on the basis of their people's wealth and opportunities. Differences in national class result largely from each nation's degree of industrialization and modernization—or from which spiral is prevalent in that land. Worldwide data indicate that there are three broad classes of nations. The upper class is composed of such nations as the United States, Canada, Japan, and Western Europe. The in-between class is composed of those countries currently going through the throes of full modernization: for example, the Soviet Union, Argentina, Peru, most Eastern European countries, and China. The lower class comprises the largely undeveloped countries, mostly in Africa and southern Asia. A host of other factors, such as average education level, gross national product per capita, infant mortality rate, and life span, highly correlate with this classification system.

These gross differences among nations are not abstract. They are raw reality—"where the rubber meets the road." In *Contemporary Social Problems*, Parrillo, Stimson and Stimson estimate that during the time it takes the average American family to eat dinner, 413 people on the planet starve to death. This won't do. One major task of the upcoming spiral will be, no doubt, for us to do something about these stark inequities as a massive collective endeavor. The alternatives are simply too bleak. Whoever says there is nothing to do!

Striving to do well is a positive human attribute, but class systems have almost always involved win-lose games in which the position of the privileged class rests on the necks of the under-privileged. As we move into a spiral of shared abundance, we may be able to leave some of this behind.

Because individuals are at many different levels of spiritual evolvement and possess widely varying skills, some kind of class structure will almost certainly continue to be part of human life. However, the human classification system could be gentler and more open to everyone, and it could be based more on such things as merit and service to humanity. Such a notion may seem utopian, even for the future, but what pharoah or medieval king would ever have believed that people would vote their leaders in (and out) of office?

Rising collective awareness will no doubt mandate massive

pharaoh or medieval king would ever have believed that people would vote their leaders in (and out) of office?

Rising collective awareness will no doubt mandate massive changes in this area. Abundance and equal *opportunities* for all humanity are the keys to a more open and fair class system.

Chapter 11

TRIBALISM

There is a peculiar subject called "Minorities" or "Race and Ethnic Relations" that is addressed by the behavioral and social sciences and is filled with controversial data. This subject graphically demonstrates how divisive humanity can be and how devastating the results of such divisiveness really are. It seems to rest upon strong remnants of the intense tribalism from earlier historical spirals and upon the major imbalances that yet plague us all.

Divisive intergroup relationships are based upon an extension of the "me versus everything else" distorted polarity into an "us versus them" distorted polarity. This divisiveness rests upon echoes from earlier tribalism, in which the name of the tribe was often the same as the word for "human being" and in which tribal feuding was a part of living that was taken for granted. *People outside the tribe were not considered human.* Even when there was no open conflict with outsiders, these nonmembers were usually discriminated against. Outsiders were looked down on because they diverged from the tribe's ways and standards. If the outsiders happened to be more powerful, the belittlement occurred behind their backs. For example, white people were often laughed at by native peoples because of their inappropriate clothing, bizarre food habits, and sexual uptightness. (In colonial Malaysia, the "natives" laughed at white people because they couldn't make love sitting up cross-legged.)

A couple of factors have accentuated like-mindedness within a tribe and differences between tribes. One is the extensive forceful socialization through which an individual learns and internalizes the ways of the group. The other is the "like attracts like" law, which leads like-minded individuals to congregate and network together. These two factors go hand in hand to produce in-group solidarity, coupled with out-group distancing and intolerance. You can test this "tropism" for yourself by considering cultures in the world to which you feel drawn and cultures for which you feel a distaste.

Variations of this tribalism are with us today in many forms that are both direct and surreptitious: neighborhood gangs, ethnic rivalry, nationalism, fierce religious sectarianism, the generation gap, the battle of the sexes, and so on. There are usually additional factors involved in these conflict situations, but tribalism is present to darkly color the interactions.

A great many people feel easy compassion only for some categories of people but not for others. Whites may feel compassion only for other whites; blacks only for other blacks; women only for other women but not for men. This is better than no compassion, but it still leaves humanity divided and at odds.

Virtually anything—any characteristic—can serve as the focus for in-group/out-group discrimination: skin color, national origin, ethnic culture, age, gender, height or size, sexual preference, religion, occupation, shape of eyes or lips. A negative stereotype of the things the group considers bad and belittling is projected onto members of the out-group, while a positive stereotype of the things considered good and admirable is projected onto in-group members. Since out-group members are considered less than fully human to a certain extent, *they can legitimately be accorded less-than-human treatment.* Of course, the members of one's own tribe come first, so the most powerful groups also establish a pecking order of privileged class positions within the society. This is the way it has been throughout most of our earlier historical spirals. We hear much about the exploitation of native peoples by colonizers, and this has certainly been true. However, long before the "white man" arrived, the Zulu, Aztecs, Samurai, and Brahmins were already busily exploiting their own out-group neighbors and underclasses. In fact, local domestic exploitations often went far beyond anything done by foreigners. For example, many African rulers sold their fellow Africans to slave traders. Also, the autocratic exploitations by many of the rajas of India of their lower caste subjects equaled anything the British came up with.

In current terminology, the groups lower down on the pecking order within a society are called "minorities" and are said to be in a "minority position." Ironically, their members are actually often the majority in terms of sheer numbers. This is true, for instance, with South African blacks, commoners during the Middle Ages, and women in most societies. These pecking orders always rest on significant differences in power and wealth. In daily living, a casual decision by a member of a privileged group can be a matter of grave concern, even life and death, to the underprivileged. ("Yes, I'll need extra porters" or "No, I think I'll close the plantation.")

Whatever the processes causing them to arise, "minority" groups are easily identified by statistics. To a greater or lesser degree, they are excluded from full participation and full opportunities within society, and this shows up in the straight facts. "Minorities" are underrepresented in positions of power, wealth, and influence, and they are overrepresented in the poverty class and among the unemployed and bankrupt. For instance, blacks, women, Hispanics, and Native Americans in the United States are very scarce as members of Congress, as federal judges, and as senior executives of major corporations. Their education levels and incomes are also significantly lower. In contemporary America, women are twice as likely as men to be poor. In the mid-1980s, there were one hundred United States senators but only two of them were women, rather than fifty; none of them were black, rather than the eleven or twelve that would have been proportionate representation. Nor were 12 percent of the Cabinet members black under the last ten presidents.

According to the U.S. Census Bureau, in the mid-1980s the median income for white families was around twenty-nine thousand dollars, while for black families it was only seventeen thousand dollars. Three times as many black families as white families were below the poverty line. Unemployment among American Indians averaged 50 percent while the national average was 6 percent. When they performed the same jobs with the same training level, women made only sixty-two cents for each dollar that men received. It is possible to go on and on and on with similar statistics.

As a society opens up, its "minorities" are often able to make it into the middle ranges of the society, but they still find great difficulty climbing into the upper reaches. For instance, in the United States, the relative position of women probably got better during the 1970s and 1980s. However, at the end of the 1980s, for every thousand males making over fifty thousand dollars annually there were only thirty-seven females, according to social researchers Parrillo, Stimson, and Stimson.

"Minorities" are usually segregated to some extent, and their movements are often controlled to some degree. This may be legal, as with modern apartheid or medieval serfs being bound to the land; in these cases, even passes to leave a segregated area have often been required. This segregation may also be informal, as in the pricing of real estate in exclusive neighborhoods. (*Anyone* can live in Palos Verdes, California, if they can afford a half-million-dollar condo or a million-dollar house.) Either way, the segregation has tended to perpetuate the position of the "minorities" through time, since it limits their easy access to the opportunities of mainstream society. The dominant groups make the rules not only for themselves but for everyone else too, and these rules have often included laws against intermarriage with the "minorities." Such rules almost always favor perpetuation of the existing pecking order.

Our scientists tell us there are no real "races." Instead, there are locales where certain genes tend to predominate. However, there has been so much mobility and interbreeding throughout the world over the millennia that every human being carries attributes from all of the major races. There are no human "purebreds." We are all hybrids.

There is a personality trait that might simply be called "degree of tolerance." Researchers have found that a person tends to be tolerant to about the same degree toward ethnic out-groups, deviants, and even made-up, nonexistent groups. For example, a person may display about the same degree of tolerance or intolerance toward Hispanics, homosexuals, and the imaginary group "Nacirema" (American spelled backwards). Therefore, any factors that help to increase individual tolerance will help to soften all intergroup relations and prejudices. When intergroup intolerance softens, people can more easily perceive their common humanity. Then there is also more balancing of the individual-interest/collective-interest polarity.

Intolerance and discrimination are human created. Through them, our perceptions of our underlying human similarities are blocked by mental-image projections of differences that make some of us "more" while making others "less." As in any massive win-lose game, the cost in human misery is high. This blockage of empathy also means that privileged members generally underestimate the starkness of the underprivileged members' conditions. The privileged are insulated from the truths of "minority" living and are often startled to discover that the "minorities" are dissatisfied.

However, the real costs go way beyond the plight of individual "minority" members. The real costs at the collective human level are the loss of the full contributions of the "minority" members to society and humanity as a whole. Where were the black and female and Native American Einsteins of the last few centuries? Picking cotton? Leading sewing circles? Perhaps they would already have given us the cure for cancer and the interstellar space drive. If all the "minority" groups are added up, America has enjoyed the full contribution of *only about 30 percent* of its population since its birth. Where would we be by now if we had had 100 percent? Cancer and the stars and the all-purpose home robot will have to wait a bit longer.

Beyond this sadness, there are some bright signs for future ethnic and "minority" relations. The massive physical and psychological mobility of our times has resulted in far greater interpenetrations among ethnic groups and "minorities" everywhere. At a superficial level, this can be seen by the rapid growth of ethnic-cuisine consumption. We taste one another's worlds in tacos, pizza, sushi, eggs Florentine, baklava, curry, egg rolls, borscht, and so on. At a deeper level, the greatly increased contacts and interpenetrations between ethnic groups are producing biological crossbreedings and cultural cross-fertilizations. Social distances between groups are declining as a result.

By itself, this increased interpenetration is not sufficient to soften ethnic relations, but other forces are also at work. Country after country has adopted a policy of *accommodation* toward its "minorities." The accommodation replaces repression with negotiation and concession. These countries are learning (often the hard way) that this is the stable win-win approach to these problems. Such accommodations are often later enacted into laws, and if their enforcement is less than perfect, they are still better than the situations they are replacing.

Therefore, many factors are now working to reduce "minority"-group inequality and segregation. Accommodation gives the "minorities" a larger share in the society's goodies. Interpenetrations are teaching the "majority" people that "minorities" are human too. This increases respect for others' ways of life. Rising awareness levels are making stark exploitations less and less acceptable, and the active strivings of the "minority" groups themselves are having moderate success around the world. The generic loosening of traditions and rigid role expectations is also melting ethnic stereotypes to some extent. Ethnic name calling has gone out of fashion.

Finally, there is the rising collective spiritual consciousness—which eventually puts an end to all false things.

Chapter 12

CHILDREN

As some readers may themselves recall, being a child throughout most of humanity's history has been a very uncertain venture. The recently documented "facts of life" about the typical circumstances of infancy and childhood in previous epochs are hard for most contemporary people to believe.

For starters, until the last couple of centuries between 20 and 30 percent of infants died within the first year of life. (The current rate is less than one percent in most industrial countries.) This figure was augmented by the common practice, widespread in the world, of abandoning unwanted babies. In most places, there was no stigma attached or crime involved in killing off unwanted children. Throughout earlier historical spirals, infanticide was the main birth-control technique. Childbearing itself was also a Russian roulette experience, in which there was a one-in-five possibility of death for the mother before her childbearing years were through.

The routine and recommended treatment of children in the past would legally qualify today as "child abuse." For example, in Europe, for many centuries, parents were admonished to "break the will" of children through harsh beatings that sometimes left the toddlers crippled for life. The idea was to crush assertiveness and instill complete obedience.

"Spare the rod and spoil the child" were words that families lived by and children sometimes died by.

Poor nutrition and sanitation levels produced stunting and slow maturation for most children, and often resulted in lives spent in underdeveloped bodies. As an example, it is estimated that the onset of puberty may have been, on the average, three years later in Medieval Europe than it typically is today. Being raised by a single parent was probably about as common in the past as it is today, but this was due to the death of one parent rather than to divorce.

According to recent research, some parents in much of preindustrial Europe and Asia did many things *wrong* for optimum child development. Lack of nurturance and physical holding produced emotional stunting. Lack of protein and minerals resulted in retarded brain and body development. (The average height of humans was several inches shorter than it is today. This is documented by the size of preindustrial body armor.) Procedures that curtailed easy movement and exploration by infants diminished motor skills and neuron development. Whole generations of children were therefore *stunted* by routine child-raising practices. Also, current experimental data demonstrate that rewards and encouragements provide a far more enriched environment for growth and self-realization than do admonitions and punishments.

We can't entirely blame the grown-ups. They were harshly raised themselves. Indifference toward children was also no doubt an emotional adjustment to the harsh conditions that often prevailed. Parents were also manifesting the collective thoughtforms prevailing in their historical spirals.

As the eminent historian Lloyd de Mause has noted, "The history of childhood is a nightmare from which we have only recently begun to awaken."

There were cultures, such as some South Sea islands and some Native American tribes, in which supportive, nurturant child-rearing practices prevailed. There were also individual parents who went against the grain in the harsher cultures and really nurtured and cared for their offspring, but they were exceptions. Our current laws against child labor, child abuse, and the sexual exploitation of children are actually very radical and very modern developments. Someone may have had a rough childhood this lifetime, with plenty of real sorrow and anguish that has been hard to release, but it was still probably a real advance over many childhoods in previous spirals. There is no question about the fact that the grim details of many earlier childhoods are among the factors occluding the easy remembrances of previous lifetimes.

In earlier spirals, and earlier phases of the present one, most children experienced far more rigid programming and control, and had far fewer choices in their lives. Today, even working-class and lower-class children have more life chances than did the vast bulk of past historical humanity. For instance, most young people can now choose their spouses and careers. These are other radical modern innovations.

We worry individually and nationally about child abuse, child education, child health, and child care for working parents. These are real transition problems. However, we have made great strides in each of these areas. The very fact that we even worry is a healthy sign that shows our rising awareness and sharply rising standards about what is acceptable.

With all the very real problems regarding children that are so widely publicized today, it might come as a surprise to realize that many children are reaching more of their potential than ever before. The fact that our ideals have now risen even higher than our accomplishments in these areas is the reason why there is such concern with the problems. In former times, there was "no problem" even as children were sold into slavery, married off for economic or political gain, controlled, indentured, conscripted, and killed if their parents didn't like their looks.

Today, in modern industrialized nations, children are less

and less locked into the ways of their parents. This is demonstrated indirectly but conclusively by the fact that fewer children retain the religious, political, or social-issue viewpoints
of their parents, as shown by many opinion polls. Two factors
seem to be at work here: changes in parents' attitudes toward
their children and the loosening of the grip of traditions.
Again, data from public opinion polls display these changes.
A half century ago, most Americans felt that "obeying parents" was the most desirable quality for a child to have; today
only around a third feel so. ("Having common sense" is now
becoming the chief desired quality.) Similar shifts are
reported in West Germany and other highly industrialized
countries.

There is another important matter regarding childhood.
For a long time, it was widely theorized that a newborn infant
was a *tabula rasa*, a blank tablet, shaped by genetics (blood)
upon which the social environment, church, and state wrote.
The child was seen as a passive item to be programmed like a
blank computer disk. This view was implicit in the work of
experimental psychologists for many decades, although a lot
of parents and sensitive people knew better. More recently, a
host of brilliantly conducted studies have demonstrated this
idea to be utterly false. As one example among many, psychologist R. Bell showed that even infants actively influence and
manipulate their care-givers. Experimental psychologists have
found strange anomalies in their results that they have termed
"autoshaping," meaning the *self-directed* modifying of one's
own conditioning and even brain structures. "Autoshaping"
was found to hold true even among pigeons. So much for classic stimulus-response theories. (Much of this data is summarized in H.W. Smith's *Social Psychology*.)

This leads to the debate over Albert Einstein's brain. Einstein donated his brain to science, and researchers have been
studying preserved bits of it since his death. They have found
an exceptionally elaborate brain structure with a very unusual

density of interconnections. Here is the debate: Did the unusual brain produce the phenomenon called Einstein? Or did the individual called Einstein produce the unusual brain? More and more hard-nosed data is supporting the latter idea.

Recent leading-edge researchers do not assert that spirituality exists (at least publicly), but implied in their work is the conception that even newborn humans are active, independent agents. This is, of course, no news to mystics or those involved in the human potential movement.

The discarnate being Seth, channeled by Jane Roberts, put it this way: "No consciousness simply reacts to stimulus; but has its own impulses toward growth and value fulfillment."

If our transition times are more child friendly than previous times, the upcoming historical spiral looks even better. Before too many years, people will have children only if they really want to—not from duty, not to prove they are real men or real women, not accidentally. *People will have children only when they want them!*

People will have fewer children. This we know, because it has happened in every country that has industrialized and modernized, whatever its religion or politics. Also, birth rates have dropped even further as countries have moved into the post-industrial transition phase. The children of these countries are more highly valued, have a more enriched environment, and have more life chances than their predecessors.

Despite all resistances, the abortion pill, which enables women to easily control their own fertility, is about to become available worldwide. This, coupled with their increasing independence, will leave women even freer to conceive children only when *they personally* wish to. *A generation in which most of the children are truly wanted will be a new and wondrous thing.*

The conditions prevailing in each historical spiral can be looked at as the "birthright" of the people born into it. The birthright of children born into the upcoming spiral may include such things as freedom from concern about any of life's necessities and increased freedom to reach their full potential for that lifetime (including freedom to "screw-off" for a lifetime). Opportunities have increased with each succeeding spiral, some of which were undreamed of by those in previous spirals. No doubt this will continue to be the case in the future.

There is a growing realization that children are not "owned" by their parents or their society—that they have their own lives and belong to themselves. This means that their natural development and their own paths will be less interfered with by (often well-meaning) adults. Like all other members of the new spiral, children will have a far richer cultural environment. Being born again won't be such an iffy prospect.

Chapter 13

WOMEN

The loosening of traditional bonds and the influences of the deep historical tides are beginning to result in the emancipation of women, which is very good news for the human race. This is a great historical shift that involves an ascension of the feminine energy principle and a great deal more besides.

Throughout recorded history, about the last five thousand years, most women have had what might be called a "shadow status." Their positions were determined first by their fathers, then by their husbands or male sexual partners. In many respects, and in some places literally, they were the property of males—sometimes indulged, but almost always dominated. There were exceptions, such as England's Queen Elizabeth, but the real point is that they *were* statistical exceptions. Also, prior to the last few decades, all the professional writings about female sexuality and intimate female problems were written by males, and they displayed all the understanding of government scientists dissecting an alien. These imbalances and stereotypes routinely colored male/female relationships, causing overweening distortions and a lot of psychic impoverishment.

Women have been a "minority" group in most times and places, with most of the underprivileges common to "minorities." They often have not been allowed to vote or own property, and usually, major life decisions were made for them by males. They were considered childlike auxiliary humans. For instance, in ancient Athens women were legally consigned to the status of children, and if they lost their virginity outside of marriage they could be sold into slavery.

Things are much better now and the trends of further emancipation are unmistakable, yet women still hold an underprivileged group position. For example, as mentioned previously, there are one hundred United States senators but only two, not fifty, of them are women. In a major state university system, women instructors of the same rank currently make several thousand dollars less than males. Women in the United States still are only a small fraction of the most prestigious professions, such as doctors, law-firm partners, senior public officials, and corporate senior executives. They are overrepresented in low-paying jobs, such as sales clerk and secretary. They are still routinely insulted in media advertisements—if you buy X, a cute squirmy girl will satisfy your sexual fantasies. A current extreme case of women's unequal status is the fact that in the Middle East and Africa there are at least seventy-five million women who have been mutilated by having their clitorises amputated. (Imagine the world outcry if it came to light that seventy-five million men had had their penises amputated!)

How insidious and deeply embedded the prejudices really are! We speak of "man" and "mankind," and "Mrs." means, literally, the possession of "Mr."

As is usually the case with "minorities," studies have also documented that women themselves are prejudiced against women. For example, women put more trust in materials allegedly written by male authors than by female authors.

However, the signs of a fundamental change from the past and its lingerings in the present are everywhere. The upcoming historical spiral could be the best times women have ever had on this planet.

In very recent times, throughout most of the world's industrial nations, women have started to become freer than they have ever been. One main trend is the increasing economic independence of women. For example, in 1900 less than one-tenth (9 percent) of American women who were married worked outside the home. By the mid-1970s, over half were gainfully employed, and this trend has been continuing. This statistic translates, for millions of women, into much increased economic independence from males. Similar or even greater changes have occurred in other modernized countries, particularly the socialist ones.

There have also been qualitative changes in women's job opportunities. Not so long ago, there were almost no women in the most prestigious professions; the jobs open to women usually involved working as subordinates for professional males, such as secretaries or nurses. By the beginning of the 1990s, however, around one-third of the law degrees and one-fourth of the medical degrees were being awarded to women. Similar increases in the proportion of women have been occurring in other prestigious, influential, and lucrative professions, such as university professorships and those requiring advanced business degrees. Now, around half the students enrolled in graduate programs are female. Increasing numbers of women are now also engaged in formerly all-male occupations such as the police, construction and welding, dock work, and assembly line supervision. These are monumental changes, and point to a very needed Womanspirit infusion into the major professions of the future. The law and medical professions could certainly use more yin (feminine) energies. The overweening dominance of male energies, at least in modernized countries, is waning.

The massive shift in cultural attitudes about women shows clearly in another statistic. In the 1930s, only around one-third of the adult American population said they would vote for a competent woman candidate for president. By the mid-1980s, this figure had risen to five-sixths of the population.

The rise in the relative position of women means that they will have an ever-growing influence upon the mass thought-forms of the emerging world society. This will help in the restoration of yin / yang balance and integration. The male principle alone tends to be brutish, although impetuous and adventurous; the female principle alone tends to be impulsive, intuitive, and nurturant. Melded together, they approach the model of the *whole* human being. These developments are not just beneficial to females—a great many men also have been suffering and languishing over the centuries due to the lack of open affinity with Womanspirit within their inner selves and in their lives. When the two poles are integrated, the polarity is vibrantly transcendent.

The loosening of the bonds of tradition has many implications for both men and women. It is causing a discernable fading of rigid gender stereotypes. Women are becoming freer to embrace a broader range of personality characteristics, such as assertiveness, formerly denied them. This loosening means they are freer to choose lifestyles, careers, habits, marital statuses, childbearing activities, sexual positions—everything. There has also been a fading of the "sex-object stereotype." ("You're cute when you get mad.") Ironically, women are now freer to treat *men* as sex objects. Women now also have no need to wait for males to call or initiate lovemaking.

Women are less and less repressed and shut away in "the female world." They are "going public" with their feelings, discontents, sexual desires, and so on. This ruffles some feathers and is sometimes a puzzle / problem for husbands, fathers, and male supervisors. However, this grass fire of self-expression is releasing generations of pent-up emotions and unsaid words. Women are putting up with less than ever.

As the bonds of tradition loosen, there is also some closing of the "social distance" between the sexes. Formerly, even married couples were often almost strangers, with each spouse drawing his or her real intimates from friends of the same sex. There was a very poor level of cross-sex communication. Recently, open communication between the sexes has been demonstrably increasing as a corollary of the other trends. This is a development in which everybody wins.

With modernization, urbanization, and women working gainfully, there has been a drop in the birth rate of every industrializing society, whatever its politics or religion. No one knows entirely why, but it seems that women in industrialized societies become more able to make decisions about their own childbearing. As they do, they decide to have fewer children. Given time, this factor alone will stabilize the world's population, perhaps at around seven billion.

There has also been a general, if partial, emancipation of women's sexuality. More and more women are becoming active partners in sex. Half a century ago, a twenty-one-year-old woman would have to hide or explain the fact that she was not a virgin. Today, if she is a virgin people wonder why. This has been a complete turnaround.

Women's biological and health situations are also being taken more seriously. The conditions of, for instance, menopause and PMS (premenstrual stress syndrome) are no longer just tossed off as female hysteria.

Things are beginning to get better for females on planet Earth. Some people might mourn the passing of male dominance, just as some mourn the passing of the cavalry charge, but the coming of the new spiral is inexorable.

According to the data from many different mystical traditions, souls, as they evolve, incorporate and distill the best from "male" and "female" energies. They are then able to manifest any desired combination of aspects from these two poles entirely by choice. Such an integration and transcendence has many implications. For instance, individuals who have integrated female and male within themselves can experience anything and everything more fully. Also, any two such beings can enjoy a more multifaceted relationship with each other, because each can play a full range of notes, so to speak. With such melding, fixed and compulsive positions such as being "macho" or being "wifey" tend to fade away.

There is no doubt that the female / male imbalances of the past have impeded individual and collective evolvement. As these imbalances ease, the future brightens. Whether a person is biologically male or female could become more incidental—and, paradoxically, more exciting.

Chapter 14

MEN

A great many people have written about the situation of women—rightfully so. However, few writers have looked at the less-than-optimum situation to which men have also been subjected throughout our history. Because they have been dominant and have had the privileges of their dominant position, it has too often been presumed that men "have it made" and therefore don't deserve much consideration. However, even though historically men have had it better than women or children, they really didn't have it so good either.

Fundamentally, there have been generations of humans who have happened to be born with male genitals who have been heavily trained and forced to become "men." A couple of decades ago, the anthropologist Jules Henry wrote a classic book entitled *Culture Against Man*. One of his main themes was that cultures are never entirely supportive of, or user-friendly for, the lives of their members. In fact, cultures can have many detrimental effects upon their people. As one example of this, the dictate to "be a man" has haunted the lives of untold numbers of human males.

The truth is, men frequently have been as trapped within the standards and sanctions of their societies as women. For one thing, their upbringings have very often left them emotional and spiritual cripples. The gentler human attributes have often been denied them and very forcibly trained out of them.

I have vivid images of living in an earlier century, a different time and place, when I was a small boy of seven. One morning before dawn I was taken from the dull security of my home and brought to a vast strange area with big wooden buildings. Nobody told me what was happening, and I was terrified. Somebody said it was the recruit barracks, but I didn't know what those words meant and I felt utterly lost in a strange place. I was whimpering when they took me and some other boys to a big muddy field. I started crying and just couldn't stop. One of the men told the other boys to shut me up, and they beat me to the ground. I lay there huddled on the ground, crying and crying in the rain and mud. Some time late in the day I just went numb inside like a stone. I went into the barracks hall and started my life as a man. Later on, yes indeed, I learned to kill with either hand. My instructors became very proud of me.

In the earlier historical spirals, most men were subjugated by the strongest male in their locale or the male with an inherited rulership. They were frequently conscripted into local feuds where they often lost their lives. Generally, they were subordinated to the arbitrary personal whims of the rulers in their area. They had few if any rights except those that were arbitrarily, and often temporarily, granted them by whoever was at the top of the pecking order.

In later spirals, the vast majority of men were utterly subordinated to hereditary rulers, and later to owners and landlords. For most males there was not much dominance involved in being miners, sharecroppers, or cannon fodder in the armies.

Throughout all the spirals, there have been men who were relatively free and successful based on their own resources or the fortunes of their births and inheritance. However, these few males were often winners at the expense of the large majority of other males, who were losers. A glorious knight, who vanquished twenty men, won by producing twenty vanquished men. We remember Lancelot in story and song, but we don't remember all the nameless men he slew.

Rigid standards prevailed throughout most of these earlier spirals. Male youths were forced to become *men*. They were called wimps, pussies, queers, or fancy boys if they didn't measure up to stern, male-chauvinist standards. This situation often produced a great deal of stress and chronic low-grade anxiety about losing their position, about being knocked off the perch—a devastating event. The lives of many men are still haunted by this "position anxiety." The rapidly increasing manifestation of Womanspirit within the collective human auric field promises to do much to alleviate this.

Males have historically been trapped in masculine energy manifestations, largely cut off from emotion and intuition. They were often pushed into games of competitiveness and macho one-upmanship. The resulting barriers also separated and distanced them from the women in their lives, even those they loved.

Men got to do more, but they had to do more. The successful were stuck in brutishness; their other chakras and attributes were repressed, resulting in diseases, shorter lifespans, and psychological problems. The epitome of total male manifestation has been approached in several cultures: the Vikings, the Apache, and the Spartans. The men in these societies had lives that were short and barren, no matter what fleeting fame they might have won.

Only in the close, male camaraderie of fellow soldiers, miners, or whatever, could men open up emotionally to some degree. This is why such relationships have often been so deep and so valued.

Men have had their secrets all along. What have men hidden from the rest of the world? Small boys, their terror. Youths, their tears. Adult males, their anxieties about making the grade. Male artists, in going against the grain, have drawn on their right-brain intuitions and yin energies, but not infrequently they have been neurotic and ill from the other imbalances.

Only during recent times have the majority of men begun to be freer to really choose their own life-courses, with fewer of the rigid constraints of traditional stereotypes binding them. They are now becoming freer to be total human beings. What a release this is! In their melding with female energy, they certainly get back far more than they give up.

As these tidal changes continue, the future promises an emergence of the new male, balanced and integrated in the polarities, and freer to step onto the moving paths of choice. This potential contains possibilities for adventure far beyond that of Siegfried or Ulysses. Eric the Red and Gawain will have a finer time.

Chapter 15

FAMILIES

The family has changed tremendously both in its overall form and in its functions as we humans have worked our way up through the historical spirals. It still remains as an intimate social grouping of sexual partners and their offspring, but otherwise it is hardly recognizable compared with what it has been in previous times. Most of the changes in the family have to do with it becoming more *voluntary* in a great many ways. The family has always changed in response to major historical changes, and it is still continuing to do so today.

Some people feel, and have loudly asserted, that most of the changes in the family are "bad." They issue dire warnings that the family will disappear altogether, with a corresponding demise of civilization. However, these judgments are moralistic, rather than factual, and they are based on adherence to traditionalism and the old world that is already gone. They are also based upon misconceptions about the facts of family living in past historical periods. There will certainly be families in the coming ages, but their future forms will almost certainly surprise us.

So many of the major human dramas and milestones of life occur within the little world of the family that it has always loomed large in the human psyche. But in our transition times, the family too has been going through some emancipations. Many facets of family life are now more voluntary than they have ever been before.

Throughout the earlier historical spirals, the family was the physical, psychological, economic, and spiritual niche within which most people experienced much of their daily lives. The family usually worked together and slept together, often in a cramped single room. It was unheard of for each person to have a separate room, except in the upper classes. In most times and places, eight or ten people might share a dwelling of four hundred to six hundred square feet—about a third the size of a modest contemporary house.

In some cultures, there was autocratic rule over the family by the eldest male, and female family members were often further despotically dominated by the eldest female. The family itself was in turn dominated by the village headman, the district supervisor, or the local lord, who could routinely interfere with the family (conscripting the men or "taking" the women) to a degree no modern nation would tolerate.

If the family was a relatively happy one, the close-knit characteristics of it made it a cozy arrangement. If it was not happy, it could be hell for the members who had few real possibilities for honorable escape from its bonds. Duty and obedience were keynotes in earlier historical spirals, whatever the cost in individual effort or misery.

If a marriage was less than fulfilling, well, that was the luck of the draw. There were strong religious and economic pressures to *endure* one's circumstances as one's lot in life. Children were sometimes treasured, but usually not, and they were often treated sternly either way. The hours of labor were long and life was usually short. Our romantic novels and movies have given us very false pictures about family life in bygone days. The popular conception of family life in these earlier times as a peaceful rural existence bonded by strong mutual affections has proven to be a myth. Love usually had little to do with marriage arrangements or the day-to-day manifestion of family life. It is primarily during our present historical spiral that romantic love has come to be accepted as the basis for creating a marriage and family. In many earlier cultures, love was actually regarded as a kind of temporary insanity. It was regarded suspiciously as a wild card that could upset "sensible arrangements." Marriage, even among the lower classes, was usually *arranged* for other reasons such as economics—not love.

All of this has now changed. Family ties have been loosened. All family members now tend to have their own worlds, their own networks of people, their own rounds of activities, and often their own rooms. Relationships among members of a family are more voluntary in form than ever before. The content and style of interactions are not prescribed by rigid cultural standards and rituals. Many of the traditional functions of the family have been taken over by outside organizations such as the public school system and the downtown workplace. More and more parents and older children work outside the home. Fewer grandparents and other relatives live under the same roof with the parents and children. Romantic love is the prevailing basis for marriage. Easy divorce has significantly changed the family game and has rescued marriage from being the life sentence it can be if things don't go well. Cohabitation and the single lifestyle have become growing major alternatives to the traditional marriage pattern in our transition times.

So what's left? A great deal, actually. For one thing, there is a greater possibility for any individual to *freely* enter into a chosen sequence of relationships with other individuals. Also, more and more people can choose to have children only if they want them and plan for them. Additionally, they can have fewer children, so that each one can be nurtured and treasured rather than just being part of a large brood. If marriages don't work very well or youths feel incompatible with their parents, the people involved are less stuck than ever before. Therefore, the unions that *do* stay together are more fulfilling. Today, *the percentage of relatively fulfilling and happy marriages and families is at an all-time high!*

The changes in the family are massive, and they are found in all industrial societies as they move into the transition times, whatever their political or religious structures.

Individualism and the ideal of individual self-realization have been emerging from the shadow of the family web. Less and less are people expected to stay within unsuccessful family situations—that is, ones that are unsuccessful in terms of self-fulfillment. In this sense, there are rising expectations of the family. For example, the traditional marriage form, with the man as the patriarchal breadwinner and the woman as the housewife, appeals to fewer and fewer women. Women's growing economic independence and career opportunities have provided them with more options and with the ability to say, "No thanks." Increasing numbers of women appear to be opting for divorce if they find themselves in downtrodden "wifey" situations.

The rise in collective expectations and awareness can be seen in another way. Wife abuse and child abuse have almost certainly *decreased* in our times; however, our awareness and standards of humaneness are increasing, causing the *perception* that abuse is increasing. "Spare the rod and spoil the child" and the law specifying the size of stick a man can use for beating his wife are just no longer acceptable. The fact that marital rape is even an issue shows our rising consciousness. No ancient Roman or Celt would have been brought before a magistrate for forcibly violating his mate. Therefore, we need to celebrate our accomplishments as well as handle our problems.

In our times, the predetermining influence of the families we are born into is fading. Once upon a time, the first thing parents would ask about some new friend or romantic interest of their child would be the newcomer's family background. They would frequently grant or deny permission for the new relationship on the basis of the answer, and this decision would stick. One hears less and less of this today, and children are freer than ever to follow their own desires, whatever their parents' responses. This is real freedom, including the freedom to make mistakes.

The greater freedom of family members can sometimes produce greater anxiety, because nobody makes arrangements for anyone else. "It's in your own hands" can sometimes be a stress-producing comment in our transition times. We are loose from the old ways, but rather untutored in the new.

The family has always been a fascinating human configuration. It has provided the grist for legends, literature, and songs since our human beginnings. As it grows out of the earlier historical spirals and moves toward a new era, it holds the promise of becoming something wondrous indeed. Futurists have focused primarily on the technological marvels of the future homestead, on the probability of more open sexuality, and on increasing collaboration on work projects. These do look like probable developments, but they may be the least of the future's wonders.

As other family functions fade, there is likely to be far more emphasis within a family on interpersonal and psychic fulfillment. As the discarnate guide Emmanuel, channeled by Pat Rodegast, has said, "The family is a hothouse for spiritual growth." The creation and flowering of families is likely to become a kind of living art form as awareness and creative ability continue to rise. Fewer compulsions and addictions will be at work, and there will be a corresponding lessening of the anguishes so common in the family life of previous epochs. There will be a lot more comforts and joys and interpersonal adventures, and a lot fewer heartbreaks.

Future family arrangements will be based more on real affinities and less on "shoulds" or duties or other bric-a brac.

Marriages may be based more on auric resonance between the partners, perhaps checked through joint bio-field readings, or on conscious, mutual karmic plans. Those choosing to incarnate into a particular family will be at higher consciousness levels, so their choices will be wiser and less obsessive. There will be more conscious spiritual awareness infusing the family and its progression through the members' incarnations. The future family may be routinely more than the sum of its parts—like a successful music group or a troop of actors.

First the Industrial Spiral and now our transition times have caused the breakup of the old family patterns that once prevailed. At the same time, they have provided the raw ingredients for future families, which may be better than any that have previously existed.

Chapter 16

SEX

Sex can feel good. It can be fun. It can be thrilling. It can be an adventure in intimacy. It can be a close physical sharing of bodily and emotional sensations between two people who love each other. Or it can be a simple satisfying action like the successful carrying out of any other physiological function, such as eating or defecating. It can be the blending of the energy fields of two spirits incarnated on the physical plane. It can be "wet and wonderful," as some of the advertisements claim. For some people it is a hobby, for others it is almost a career.

Sex can, however, also be a source of frustration and anguish. Sexual failures can engender heartbreak and the most abject and intractable sorts of grief. Sex can be an unpleasant duty. Or even if pleasant in the doing, it can produce subsequent feelings of guilt and shame and being "soiled" or "tainted." People have not infrequently languished and committed suicide (dramatically or slowly) over a lack of it or because they have done it. People have desperately sought it in the hope that it would be some kind of personal salvation.

We have great and haunting sexual stories—sometimes tragic, as in Romeo and Juliet, and sometimes joyous, as in

Richard Bach's *The Bridge Across Forever.* However, these stories have not represented the common experience of most of
humanity in most times and places.

People have given sex to others as a reward or even out of
kindness. People have traded sex for every imaginable kind of
goods and services, from meals and places to stay to classified
information or parts in movies. People withhold sex from
others as a form of interpersonal punishment, and promise
sex to others as a form of interpersonal manipulation.

Sex is a laughing matter—anthropologists have found
that every culture informally practices sexual joking. ("These
two water buffalos were. . ."). Sex is not a laughing matter—if
you have the wrong kind of sex or have it with the wrong person or under the wrong circumstances, you can have your
reputation irrevocably ruined, or you can be exiled or jailed or
mutilated or unpleasantly killed.

Sex intermittently haunts our dreams and daydreams—
and nightmares. When we're into sex it may be overwhelming
and all-consuming; when we're not into sex it may seem like a
somewhat silly and dangerous game. Sex is capable of energizing both the highest and the lowest emotional-energy
wavelengths. Throughout our sequences of lifetimes, sex has
often been a major facet of our negative and positive karmic
bonds with others.

Sex also involves an interpenetration of the vibrational
energies and psychic auras of the partners. In her therapeutic
work, Chris Griscom found that these field linkages usually
last at least forty-eight hours. There are similar field linkages
during sensual dream contacts.

Taking all these points together, it is apparent that sex has
had a powerful influence on individual and collective human
evolutionary history. On a deeper level, it is also obvious that
the major polarity imbalances examined in this book have
been plaguing people's sex lives for a long time.

The detrimental effects of the male / female imbalance are

fairly obvious. They create a gulf between the biological sexes that impedes open, flowing sexual communication and many other sorts of interpersonal interchanges. Because of the blockage in flow between male and female, the sexes are *segregated* from one another, even though they may be sleeping together in the same bed. The dominance of male energies has also led to the subjugation and exploitation of women rather than to a balancing and mutually enriching energy interchange. The most extreme form of this imbalance is forcible rape, but the far more widespread form is the culturally enforced women's role of pleasing and serving men. There have been a great many societies in which some of the female population have been trained in the arts of pleasuring men. However, there have been far fewer societies in which men have been trained to sexually satisfy women. Nowhere is the handiwork of our gross imbalances more evident than in the area of human sexuality. The price of this imbalance is high—too high.

A young child is forced into one gender category or the other and is thereafter intensively trained and admonished to stay there throughout his or her lifetime. We might as well have him or her go through life one legged, one armed, and one eyed.

The self-interest/collective-interest imbalance is also at work in the area of sex. Because of Western culture's individualistic bias, a great many people are literally "self-ish" when it comes to sex. Since a major facet of heightened sexual experience arises from free-flowing energy interchanges, the effects of this blockage are immediate and extensive, resulting in the various so-called sexual inadequacies and in difficulties in achieving real sharing and orgasmic release. Self-ishness creates a kind of psychological and spiritual isolation, whether one is surrounded physically by others or not. And it creates a sort of sexual isolation, whether one is with a partner or not.

You can sometimes "catch yourself" in the throes of this

self-interest / collective-interest imbalance in the following way. As Western-scientist-turned-Eastern-mystic Ram Dass points out in *Be Here Now*, we often have compassionate, charitable, or sharing impulses toward others, but immediately our computations of caution, fear of involvement, "What's in it for me?" or self-serving egotism enter in, either coloring or short circuiting the original impulses. Needless to say, this curtails spontaneous interactions with others, sexual or otherwise.

Sexual problems related to the imbalance in the materialism / spirituality polarity are more subtle but equally detrimental. The absence of "spirit" in sex tends to reduce it to a matter of mechanics. This is a main source of post-coital letdowns. Many current sex manuals have a basic flaw of being long on technique and short on helping to create the real sensualities, which rest upon spiritual energies. Techniques are not *live*. They can be important, but by themselves they do not make music. The importance of inspiration and artistic rendering over technique exists in all of the performing arts.

Historically, hardly any area has been as bound down with the barriers of norms, values, fixed ideas, and vested interests as sex. (Religion has possibly been the only area to exceed it.) Possessiveness in sexual relationships is so rampant it is taken for granted, despite the deeper truth that no one can possess another soul. The vested interests of males have become so entrenched that they are part of our collective reality. Generations upon generations of churchmen have shaken their fingers at us in admonition. Well, it's time to be freer.

In the throes of such distortions, our sexual maladies have sometimes even been exalted as "virtues." As Marilyn Ferguson, author of *The Aquarian Conspiracy*, wrote, "Leery of trusting the promise of an oasis, we defend the merits of the desert." Collective humanity has sometimes admired celibacy, those who have kept "their minds above their belly buttons," and people, especially women, who have not harbored "dirty thoughts." As part of a generalized avoidance pattern, sex, genital fluids, and menstrual flows have been defined as "dirty." In such a social and psychic atmosphere, many people have been flatly ashamed of their sexual desires and even of the fact that they possess genitals. Even married couples who have had several children and have lived together for decades might never have seen each other naked. An example of a related social phenomenon is that tablecloths used to be widely used, in part, to cover the "bare legs" of dining tables.

Despite all of these and other problems, sex has, throughout the ages, frequently been a source of simple pleasure and an avenue for intimate bonding between individuals. In our transition times, we are yet a long way from full emancipation in the area of sex. Yet, many aspects of sex are freer than they have been before, and there are fewer stigmas surrounding the subject of sexuality.

Modernization has also greatly increased our sexual knowledge. We now know more about the physical act of sex than we ever have. We know how our bodies function during sex, and how sexual dysfunctions can be relieved. This knowledge has been a boon to the entire field. For example, most men historically didn't even know the clitoris existed (and many women didn't either, amazingly enough). Now this knowledge is widely available in popular sex manuals and sex-education courses.

At the holistic and spiritual levels, the human potential movement has also come to the aid of sex. As people's energies become more open and expansive, and as they awaken spiritually, there tends to be a rise in their sensuality. The capacity to experience and enjoy sex increases with the capacity to experience and enjoy everything else. This does not mean "free love" or promiscuity—it simply means more freedom and capacity in the area of sexuality. This can be seen on many different fronts. Public opinion polls show a steady increase in the percentage of Americans who accept premarital sex and sexual experimentation. This can be seen in the fading of condemnation of those who are sexually active, however the activity is expressed. It can be seen in the more open discussion of sexual matters in the media and in informal conversations. It can be seen in the fact that fewer people feel that it is necessary to be "in the closet" about their sex lives. It can be seen in our movies, novels, magazines, and music.

In more recent times, AIDS has come along to darken the picture of sex to some degree. The risk of contracting AIDS and its rapid diffusion throughout the world have caused people to reexamine where they stand on sex. The disease will have to be mastered; otherwise, there is virtually no limit to its eventual spread. Elisabeth Kübler-Ross, the Mother Teresa of the New Age movement, feels that AIDS is giving humanity a chance to learn love and compassion on a mass basis. However this may be, "safe sex" is certainly the thing to practice. Whatever develops concerning AIDS, it certainly will not stop our growing collective sophistication and emancipation regarding sex.

Past-life therapists routinely find that there is a great deal of encysted emotion and low-wavelength energy locked up in sexual matters and misadventures. Both individually and collectively, there seems to be much accumulated sexual residue from earlier times. The increased openness in our own era is probably allowing a great deal of this accumulation to dissipate. This alone will significantly lighten the psychic fields of planet Earth. If this is the case, we can expect that, in our future lives, sex and sensuality and physical love will be better than ever.

Chapter 17

LIFE SPAN

At first glance, the connections between human life span and our future lives may not be obvious, but they are actually quite extensive. From the viewpoint of raw statistics, these connections begin to come clear.

In earlier historical spirals, the prevailing age distribution in the human population consisted of many young people, a moderate number of adults, and not very many oldsters. Also, members of the lower classes lived, on the average, only half as long as those of the upper classes. However, the average age of populations has been steadily increasing throughout history. In America, around 1820 the median age of the population was 16.7 years. By 1900 it had risen to 24 years. Now the median age is over 33 years.

During the last two centuries, widespread improvements in sanitation, nutrition, and medical technology have cut the annual death rates in half or more throughout most of the world. For instance, in the United States, even as late as 1900, the average life expectancy was only 47 years; nine decades later it has become 75 years. (At the time of the signing of the Declaration of Independence, it was only 35 years.)

Now, for the first time ever, there is a stretching out of the "age pyramid." The percentage of people in the older age cat-

149

egories is swelling. For example, the percentage of people over 65 in the United States has increased more than fourfold during the twentieth century. An even more startling figure is that, according to the United States Census Bureau, in 1964 there were only 527 people over 100 years old in the United States. In 1989, there were over 25,000—a fiftyfold increase. Similar trends are happening in all industrial societies, and we are only beginning to realize what they may mean.

The length of the average incarnation has doubled. It's as if most of us have been bequeathed a "grace period" of thirty to forty extra years on the physical plane. Coupled with other developments, this means a great many things. One is that a growing number of the people in the world are experiencing more than one career and more than one family of some type or another. They are living in several different geographic locales during one lifetime and are having the time to sample many different perspectives. More of us are also experiencing all the stages of life rather than having our incarnations cut short. Because of these factors, a significant acceleration of individual and collective evolvement is probably occurring.

Bodies, like everything else on the physical plane, *do* wear out. But this wearing out is greatly hastened if a person has poor nutrition and sanitation, a violent and capricious environment, and impoverished surroundings. Many studies have demonstrated that people (and all other living things) wilt or bloom depending on whether their environments are stark or enriched. The negative environmental factors are easing for a larger and larger proportion of Earth populations. Also, we are learning to intervene, both with conventional medicine and with holistic and spiritual technologies, to further stretch our life spans.

There is every reason to believe that these positive trends will continue into our future lives. Looming ecological imbalances and major planetary upheavals might temporarily reverse them. However, the underlying forces that have pro-

LIFE SPAN 151

duced them and the basic technical data on sanitation, nutrition, medical-corpsman-level medicine, and the newer alternative health approaches are now so widespread that they could not possibly be lost—they are known to millions.

Until very recently, there were a lot of misconceptions and negative stereotypes floating around in our society about older people, for instance that they were nonsexual, "set in their ways," and childish. The facts, revealed by extensive recent research, are blowing many of these myths away—and once again the truth is more heartening than the mass thoughtforms were. Older people themselves are actively redefining what it means to be a senior citizen (just as teenagers have done for their age group in recent decades). In the process, rigid expectations are fading, to everyone's great relief.

One myth that is being washed away is that people become virtually nonsexual after middle age. The truth is that sexual patterns *change* after middle age, but they certainly don't disappear. There can, in fact, be a growth in sensuality (as opposed to lust), particularly if there is a progressive opening up of the body's energy centers (chakras). It turns out that the majority of people over sixty-five are sexually active, and many pursue romantic adventures with all the zest of adolescents.

Another myth that is falling by the wayside is that older people are more conforming than youths. Research has shown that in fact the opposite is true. Older people are more independent in their judgments and beliefs, and young people are much more vulnerable to peer-group pressures. As Maggie Kuhn, founder of the Grey Panthers, has said, those of us who are old can afford to live dangerously.

A third stereotypical myth is that people have done all their basic development and learning by the age of twenty-one and that there is a slow downhill deterioration from there on out. Many studies (summarized in Michael Hutchison's

Megabrain) demonstrate that this is not the case at all. Indeed, given an enriched intellectual environment, it seems that the human brain can regenerate and expand, even at age seventy. The fact that more and more people are launching entirely new careers after age fifty further demonstrates this. There is also growing evidence that inductive abilities *increase* with age.

How about happiness? Again, there is a surprise. An excellent National Opinion Research Center study found that people over sixty-five were, on the average, the *happiest* age group. About 30 percent of those under sixty-five said they were "very happy," but this figure rose to almost 40 percent among those over sixty-five. Over 50 percent of those over sixty-five who were still married reported themselves very happy— the highest percentage of any category. Another surprise was that people over sixty-five were almost twice as likely as younger people to be "pretty satisfied" with their present financial situation. These are, of course, only averages, and there are indeed other older people who are sick, poor, and isolated. However, the overall picture painted by these figures is quite different from the negative public stereotypes.

There is another factor about life spans that might be the most important one of all. So far, there is only anecdotal evidence for this, but many experts and visionaries have asserted that spiritual awakening most typically happens to people during and after mid-life. The fact that more and more people are living to this point may have untold implications for our future lives, our collective evolution, and the prevailing atmosphere of the upcoming spiral.

Whatever the implications, the doubling of our life spans certainly gives us a longer time to "work things out." It probably also means an acceleration of the spiritual evolutionary process, both individually and collectively. Also, it would seem to be much more efficient.

As the percentage of older people continues to increase,

their influence on society will continue to grow. If this segment does in fact contain increasing numbers of spiritually awakened people, the influences will be beneficent and far reaching.

How many years the average life span will extend in the upcoming spiral is anybody's guess. Because bodies are physical objects, there may well be an upper limit to the extension. However, it is entirely feasible to estimate that it may double again. This would certainly make life a new game.

Wisdom has often been considered an attribute of age. So who knows—we may be having more wisdom abroad in the world.

Chapter 18

POPULATION

Our current world population explosion is a simple story. It is the result of the relationship between two simple statistics: the birth rate, or the number of live births per year per thousand people, and the death rate, or the number of deaths per year per thousand people. World population size has always been very intimately connected with the prevailing historical spiral. This is true today and will be true for the upcoming era. There could possibly exist *tens of billions* of humans as the next spiral comes into full blossom. For this to happen, it is only necessary for us to become a space-faring species.

The conditions prevailing during each spiral have been the major determinants of how large the human population could be. During the arduous conditions of the Hunting and Gathering Spiral, a high birth rate was balanced by a very high death rate, so communities remained small and scattered, and the total population low. Death was a fairly constant risk, especially for the young and the old. To some degree, there was a real "survival of the fittest" factor at work, and even a moderate shift in environmental conditions might have been disastrous. During the Agricultural Spiral, the food surpluses and the more stable lifestyle allowed for large population increase and the growth of empires in Egypt, Peru, China, and elsewhere. However, it was not until the technologies of the Industrial Spiral that there was an exponential growth in population. At the same time, ironically, this industrial lifestyle has set in motion the factors that will soon be halting this rapid growth, at least within the biosphere of the planet itself.

During the early historical spirals, a significant population increase did not necessarily mean that the *quality of life* for most people was that much better. There is growing evidence that one of the factors clouding people's memories of early previous lives is the fact that these lives were frequently less than joyous. For the bulk of humanity, early lifetimes were squalid and numbing, with occasional trauma thrown in for variety. It is not accidental that the religious hymns and folk music of so many cultures have embodied the theme of yearning for release from physical life, which was considered to be "a vale of tears." "I am a poor wayfaring stranger, traveling through this world of woe." "If it wasn't for bad luck, I'd have no luck at all." No doubt these harsh conditions also contributed to short life spans, wherein spirits opted out of incarnations. Life in an ancient copper mine, or chained below decks as a slave rower on a galley, or in the dull, grueling situation of a scratch farmer could stimulate feelings of "to hell with this" and "I'm out of here."

In the early stages of the Industrial Spiral, three factors came into play that drastically reduced the death rate, often cutting it by more than half. The first of these was the widespread introduction of sanitation procedures such as the chlorination of water, the disposal of sewage, and sterilization techniques performed by health personnel for themselves and their instruments. The second factor was improved nutrition as the standard of living rose somewhat. The third factor involved advances in rudimentary medical technologies, such as innoculation against virulent contagious diseases. However, it was still the normal, accepted practice at this time to have large families. Since death rates dropped dramatically, while birth rates remained high, there was a great surge in population numbers.

In these earlier spirals, just about everybody was in favor of lowering death rates—but not so birth rates. Cultures contained strong standards favoring lots of babies, and men and women were expected to prove their manliness and womanliness by being fruitful. ("Be fruitful and multiply.") These standards were often reinforced by compulsions from previous incarnations to have lots of children as an insurance policy against scarcity. Such past-life compulsions can be entirely out of phase with current conditions, much like a modern, nuclear-age general who has memories of being an infantry officer and commands, "Give them a taste of powder and shot."

In today's later stages of the Industrial Spiral, however, other forces have come into play to begin transforming the mass thoughtforms about fertility. For the first time in history, we are beginning to have low birth rates in the most modernized countries.

In every nation that industrializes and modernizes, the birth rates begin to drop. No one knows all the reasons why this occurs, although there is much speculation about it. When countries urbanize, small families become the preferred pattern, whatever the society's political or religious beliefs. In the typical urban setting, children become an economic liability rather than an economic asset. Estimates are that it now costs around $140,000 to raise and fully nurture a middle-class child in America. In addition, the involvement of women in the labor force has both interfered with women bearing a large number of children and decreased women's interest in having many children. Also, people today generally marry later than they did in earlier times. Then there is the factor of vastly improved birth control technology, which has been made widely available to the populace. In our transition times, having a child is becoming a negotiated, planned event rather than an "act of nature." Our world is indeed changing.

There are many problems regarding population that won't go away soon. Many Third World countries are simply drowning in people, most of whom are young and dependent. This keeps the average standard of living depressed and also puts immigration pressures on the better-off nations. It directly or indirectly dilutes the quality of life for the entire human race. (For instance, through partial loan defaults, emergency aid, and other mechanisms, foreign population problems cost the average American taxpayer several hundred dollars a year.)

In a brilliant sociological research study, Gove, Hughes, and Galle found that crowding resulting from population density can have many detrimental social and psychic effects. They found that when a home had more than one person per room, members were less satisfied with family life. There were more family fights and less marital satisfaction, child care was poorer, and the members tended to withdraw physically and emotionally. I might add the speculation that in crowded conditions people's auric fields are continually mushed together, so that individuals have little psychic space of their own.

With such overcrowding and resultant resource scarcities, some very cruel population control factors enter the picture: famine, disease, economic depression, and war. These cruel factors prevailed as "population control" devices in earlier historical spirals, but they no longer need to do so. The barriers examined in the Dark Side chapter are now the only thing preventing a good life for everyone.

An often neglected aspect of population pressure is that it increases various kinds of environmental problems. The burning of fossil fuels for warmth, industry, and transportation by billions of people, for instance, contributes heavily to the increasing pollution of the atmosphere. Also, the vastly increased use of artificial pesticides and fertilizers to grow food for a hungry world is polluting the water tables of the entire planet. These excesses are "theoretically" unnecessary, but our major imbalances and barriers are at work here, too, to perpetuate them.

Our process of completing the current Industrial Spiral and making the transition to the next spiral can be seen in the mass thoughtforms prevailing in different cultures. In parts of Africa, where the Industrial Spiral has hardly begun, the preferred number of children, by survey, is over seven. In the developing countries of Asia, it is four. In the developed transition nations it is two. These prevailing mass thoughtforms are the main determinants of what happens with population growth. They are more crucial than any religious pronouncements or government policies. When people don't want to have large families, they don't have large families. Despite the alarmist reports, birth rates have begun substantially declining in almost all Third World countries in recent years—thus defusing the so-called "Population Bomb." According to 1983 U.S. Census data, birth rates have been declining since 1960 on all the continents of the world except Africa. The more modernized the continent, the greater the decline. Ordinary people aren't as dumb as social scientists sometimes think they are.

There is also an emerging characteristic of population that is brand new in history. In all earlier historical spirals, the largest proportion of the population was children, the next largest proportion adults, and the lowest proportion older people. Now, for the first time, the relative proportion of older people is rapidly expanding. Within the next generation, the median age in post-industrial societies is likely to reach forty. What does this mean? Who really knows? It has never happened before. One thing it will mean is a further eventual slowing of population growth, since older people have fewer children.

This stretched-out age structure will be one of the facts of life in the upcoming spiral.

Individually and collectively, we are beginning to learn how to live with our new situations. We are accumulating more awareness and knowledge about the "facts of life" of post-industrial society. The average consciousness level of humanity is rising. As these factors increase in influence, there are already the signs of a gradual diminishing of our obsessive behavior about procreation. We no longer need to breed like flies.

Based on these signs, we can expect a leveling off of planet Earth's human population size within the next century. However, simultaneously we can expect a mushrooming of the total human population as we move into space. The idea that space could soon be massively colonized is just incredible and unbelievable to a great many transition people, but a great many things that are a routine part of our transition life, such as cars, commuter jets, computers, and worldwide television, would have been unbelievable to almost all the people living at the turn of the present century. The unfolding of history is always surprising. A few more technological breakthroughs, and humanity is in space on a mass basis.

Chapter 19

HEALTH

With each succeeding historical spiral, the overall health of human beings has dramatically improved. There is much worry today about the great killers—heart disease and cancer. Yet this concern misses the fact that, for the first time in history, the majority of people are *living long enough* to even be susceptible to these diseases, for they are diseases whose incidence increases with age.

There are many twists to the story of health on the physical plane. Good medical technologies, for example, were sometimes developed in earlier epochs, then lost, then rediscovered. For instance, traditional Chinese medicine helped produce the largest population in the world during the Agricultural Spiral, but this medical system has been regarded in the West as superstition and quackery until recently. Another twist in the story of health is that while people today enjoy unprecedented levels of health, we are suffering gravely from the polarity imbalances and negativities examined earlier—to the point that these are probably the major causes of death, underneath the more superficial symptomatic causes that are so widely publicized. Younger people today look forward to living longer, but they harbor a major negative thoughtform—a fear of the diseases of aging that they observe in older people.

Through careful analysis of historical documents and some very sophisticated statistical techniques, researchers such as Ivan Illich have found three main factors that have led to the health improvements of our current spiral. The first of these is sanitation. This involves such things as the disinfection of drinking water, the disposal of sewage, more room in houses so that people aren't continually infecting one another, washers, dryers, dishwashers, showers, and sterile procedures used by midwives and doctors for themselves and their instruments. In earlier centuries, people seldom bathed or changed their clothes. Even fifty years ago, most people changed their underwear and bathed only once a week, so they were walking bacterial hosts. The daily shower is a very modern innovation, as are clean diapers.

The second factor is nutrition. Those nations firmly established in the Industrial Spiral began to enjoy a significant rise in the average standard of living that has included a better diet, including a wider variety of nutritious foods such as fruits, vegetables, and proteins, especially important for small children. It is true that we have problems with refined sugars and junk foods, but we still enjoy a great improvement over the poor, plain diets that most people had to subsist on a few centuries back. There were particular geographical enclaves, such as parts of China and certain islands, where people ate very well, but these were exceptions. Because of modern worldwide transportation systems and preservation technology, even low-income Americans can go to the supermarket and buy foods of a variety unparalleled in history.

Today there is also better quality control of the food available. Poisoning and infectious diseases, spread through contaminated foodstuffs and water, used to be quite common and periodically resulted in plagues that ravaged the populace. Now such contamination is quite rare and newsworthy.

(Although today we have chemical contamination instead.) Government control of ingredients and safe food-preservation processes is a major human accomplishment. There are scandals in these areas, for instance, in the actual quality of government meat inspection, but this situation is still much better than no inspection at all.

The third factor leading to significant health improvements is medicine, especially routine medical procedures, such as vaccinations and antibiotics, and emergency medical systems. There is good evidence that this factor is actually the least significant of the three, despite all the claims of the medical establishment. Life expectancies greatly expanded because of improved sanitation and nutrition *before* the advent of modern high-tech medicine.

In our transition times, there exist in Western countries three major belief structures or paradigms regarding health and healing. There is the conventional scientific medical model, practiced by the overwhelming majority of Western doctors and hospitals. There is the holistic approach, practiced by a small number of doctors and by a rapidly growing host of alternative health professionals. Finally, there is the spiritual model, which treats illness as the result of some kind of spiritual travail or blockage. These three belief systems can blend with one another, although they are distinct.

For the last few decades, the conventional medical perspective, with its strong Newtonian emphasis on mechanical intervention in body processes through drugs and surgery, has dominated. This is partly due to its successes. For instance, millions of people who would have seen poorly, if at all, two centuries ago, see well today due to eye surgery and eyeglasses. Millions of people still have their teeth because of tremendously improved dental technology. The routine use of antibiotics has also saved millions of lives. And where else would you go to get a broken bone properly set or a deep cut properly treated?

However, there is another, darker side to the dominance of the conventional medical model. It arises partly from the imbalances discussed earlier and partly from the propaganda of the medical establishment and the multinational drug corporations. Conventional medicine is Big Business, with its own fixed ideas and entrenched vested interests. In the United States (as opposed to almost all other industrial countries) health care is still a commodity for sale. (If you have enough money you can live.) And the price keeps going up. Today, an illness can cost as much *with* insurance as it used to cost a person *without* insurance. A sick American faces a double trauma—the trauma of the illness plus the crisis of somehow financing the treatments. This is definitely not user-friendly health care.

This paradigm also fits hand-in-glove with the old-world Newtonian perspective that humans are only complex biological machines and that strictly physical processes are the basis of life. It virtually ignores or contemptuously dismisses all the ancient and modern evidence about mental and spiritual influences upon human illness or health.

A number of doctors themselves have been the whistle-blowers and the strongest "inside story" critics of conventional medicine. Perhaps the most famous among these is Dr. Robert Mendelsohn, a renowned veteran physician and medical-school instructor. In *Confessions of a Medical Heretic*, he wrote, "I believe that ninety percent of Modern Medicine could disappear from the face of the earth—doctors, hospitals, drugs, and equipment—and the effect on our health would be immediate and beneficial." He goes on to document how a large proportion of surgeries are unnecessary, mutilating, and dangerous; how pregnancy has become viewed as a "sickness" to be elaborately treated; and how even diagnostic testing is often an uncalled-for, hazardous venture. These may seem like extreme claims, but Mendelsohn presents impressive evidence to back them up.

A more balanced view is presented in Dr. Bernie Siegel's wonderful book, *Love, Medicine, and Miracles,* which contains many cases of "miracle" healings of grave illnesses that defy conventional medical viewpoints.

The conventional medical perspective has an almost overwhelming influence in current industrial societies. It is a collective mass thoughtform that is programmed into the populace, to the point where it is taken for granted by very large numbers of people. It is something of an automatic response: if one is not feeling too well, one goes to see a doctor. This is a phenomenon that social scientists have termed "the medicalization of society." As a result of this phenomenon, more and more situations that arise in the process of living, such as rambunctious kids or an obsessive thirst for alcohol or the teenage blues, are coming to be defined as medical problems and the domain of doctors. For example, hundreds of thousands of "hyperactive" children and millions of personally upset women are now routinely given doctor-prescribed tranquilizers. The success rates of such programs are very questionable, but the programs are very profitable for doctors and drug companies.

We also have in our times a new phenomenon: the chronic consumers of conventional medical technology—the medical junkies. These are people who become hooked on conventional medical processes as solutions to their various and sundry problems and their unreleased coarse-emotion energies. They may spend decades haunting the waiting rooms and operating rooms and pharmacies of the medical establishment as part of a dependency syndrome. The "fixes" they receive are only partially successful and often become more elaborate over time. There are certainly legitimate circumstances in which individuals need fairly continual medical care, but one wonders if the addition of alternative health procedures might not help alleviate even these situations. There are volumes of evidence now that such holistic alternatives can often break these vicious cycles of dependency on conventional medical techniques.

There is another ominous situation with regard to health care in the United States. Alone among Industrial Spiral nations, the United States and South Africa do not have national health-care programs. U.S. citizens pay more than anyone else for health care but get less for their money, and some critics assert that the American consumer is being swindled. Americans are spending approximately one-eighth of the entire Gross National Product on health care, yet the majority of nations with socialized medical programs have achieved longer average life expectancies and lower infant mortality rates than the United States—and they have shorter hospital stays and perform fewer surgeries. For instance, the infant mortality rate in Japan is around six per thousand, but it is eleven per thousand in the United States.

A person might say, well, I don't use doctors much so I'm not paying these high bills. But here is another example of an unseen collective interest at work. Skyrocketing medical costs are passed on to the general consumer in many indirect ways. For instance, because of medical benefit programs, it is estimated that health-care costs add around six hundred dollars to the price of every new car. Medical insurance costs are a hidden percentage of the price of most consumer products and services. Every time a person in the United States buys a loaf of bread, part of the money goes toward the medical insurance programs of the companies involved in producing and selling the bread. Medical costs are also a portion of everyone's local, state, and federal tax liabilities.

There are, however, many other more positive things going on that are the first intimations of what health care could become in the upcoming historical spiral. Because of public pressures about its excesses and because of research developments, conventional medicine itself is slowly becoming more benign. New techniques hold the promise of being less invasive and more effective; laser surgery, PET scanning, and physical therapy are all good signs. Also, portions of the medical profession are beginning to draw on other traditions such as imaging and acupuncture. However, the basic mechanistic paradigm remains pretty much intact and dominant.

The biggest health news in recent years is the rapid growth in alternative health approaches. These are beginning to produce a basic shift in how the whole field of disease and health is perceived. They encompass a host of perspectives and techniques, ranging from nutrition and chiropractic to extremely esoteric spiritual systems. This growth is a grassroots ground swell, and it is occurring in the face of fierce, concerted opposition from the entrenched medical establishment.

Holistic-health professionals occupy something of a middle ground between conventional medicine and more far out spirituality. They treat the entire human configuration of body, mind, spirit, and environment, and strive for wellness and exuberance rather than merely the absence of sickness. The vast majority of holistic-health practitioners would subscribe to the contention that there is a psychosomatic element to all illness. They like to spell disease "dis-ease." They seek factors beyond biological ones that predispose a person toward sickness and prolong its course. They often blend good science with trained intuition in their practices. Holistic professionals know something important: Doctors can heal people whom shamans can't, but shamans can heal people whom doctors can't.

The most "far out" approaches to health care, yet the ones that may come to predominate in the new era, are spiritually based. They have an utterly divergent perspective on the human condition from the mechanistic medical model, and therefore their techniques are utterly divergent. However, a tiny proportion of traditional medical doctors—Richard Gerber, Bernie Siegel, and others—are beginning to bridge the gap between the two paradigms.

One underlying belief of spiritually based health-care systems is that humans are fundamentally spiritual beings, so the prime cause of their misadventures is spiritual, not physical. This spiritual cause may involve spiritual anguish of some sort or another, or it may involve a lack of connectedness with spirituality. A second basic premise of spiritually based systems is that all portions of the living cosmos, including humans, act and interact through vibrational-energy interchanges. The shape people are in spiritually and the kinds of energies they routinely "bathe in" are seen as determining factors influencing their health level, whatever their symptomatic factors may be. From these two premises, spiritually based therapies involve ameliorating people's travails or adjusting their vibrational energies and releasing blockages. Successful treatments are sometimes miraculous from the mechanistic viewpoint.

This spiritually based perspective rests on the fact that *the body is ordinarily healing itself all the time* and if it is not doing so, there are spiritual-energetic reasons that must be addressed for any real healing to occur. Spiritual workers consult and work in partnership with the "inner physician" within each person on the premise that all healing is, at least in part, self-healing. As Bernie Siegel puts it, "Healing is always an inside job." With each passing year, the techniques for helping the body heal itself are becoming more refined, documented, and widely disseminated. Perhaps in a more enlightened future year they will be taught to all school children.

Professionals working with the spiritual perspective have uncovered what has turned out to be simultaneously the gravest public-health menace facing our planet and the most promising possibility for improved health in our transition times and future lives. This factor is psychic pollution, a problem that extends even into the lower astral levels.

To put it simply and baldly, the current collective vibrational fields of this planet are unhealthy! Some of these fields and mass thoughtforms are negative, some are limiting, and some are holding in place our major imbalances and barriers. A good many of these negative energies have been carried forward from previous historical spirals and represent "unfinished business" for the human race, individually and collectively. These energies are "in the air," like psychic smog, and their effects are even more widespread and insidious than physical pollutants. They are in the streets if you go out, and they often arrive with the mail if you stay in.

Truth to tell, we go around "sickening" one another or helping heal one another all the time. "He makes me sick" can have a tragic literal meaning, but, happily, "I feel good being around her" can also be literally true.

Vibration levels have been worse than today's in particular times and places. For instance, during massive plagues, the psychic atmosphere consisted of numbness and terror, and perhaps a third of the population died. During drawn-out wars, brutalization and apathy infected even the foliage and animals.

Mass negative thoughtforms create a situation that is like bathing in dirty dishwater—or bathing in one's own sewage. Some people flee to temporary safe spots or retreats of some sort. However, many more are entranced, under a spell, within the cloudy swirls, hoping that a bit of material security or sexual pleasure or narcotizing substance will rescue them from their anxieties. Or, they hope that the doctors with their gleaming apparatuses and magic potions will handle anything that goes really wrong. Fat chance.

There is now rapidly growing empirical evidence to back up the importance of the spiritual perspective. For example, in 1989 the University of Michigan Institute of Social Research released the results of a massive study summarizing twenty years of individual researchers' work and found that adults who live alone and have few social contacts are significantly more likely to suffer health problems and die prematurely. They found that social isolation is as significant to mortality rates as smoking, high blood pressure, high cholesterol, obesity, and lack of physical exercise. It also turns out that a worker's job satisfaction, including his or her psychic work atmosphere, probably has more to do with longevity than medical treatments. Psychic pollution is also a major contributor to *mental* illness. A life without love, laughter, and affection is very likely to be a short life.

One of the main problems with psychic pollution is its vicious cycle of chronic "re-infection" that affects large segments of the populace. For example, you might feel good in the morning and kindly toward others, but then you read a newspaper filled with death and destruction or you run into an upset on the job that plummets you back into the coarser vibration levels, and suddenly queasiness and ill humor become the order of the day. You might then spread the psychic pollution by acting from these coarser vibration levels toward the others in your environment and toward your own body. Our bodies *do* wear out, like any physical-plane objects, but these psychic pollutions produce premature and unnecessary deteriorization and trashing.

Well, now for the good news. There are rapid advances being made within all three health-care perspectives, and there are signs of more bridges between them as well as integrations of their approaches. This means we can virtually count on another leap in improved health in our future lives.

Within conventional medicine, researchers are at last delving into the body's deep immunological systems. Also, partly because of mounting public pressure, there is now a concerted search in medicine for less violent, less invasive, and less expensive testing and treatment procedures. There is also a growth in awareness about the important effects of the patient's mindset and heart-set upon illness and recovery. Theoretically, there is no reason a patient has to be half-killed to be treated, and even the mechanistic-approach practitioners are beginning to grasp this.

In the last few decades, the holistic-health-care approach has grown from the ideas of a scattering of "oddballs" like the venerable heretic author of *Food Is Your Best Medicine*, Dr. Henry Bieler, and the founder of chiropractic, B.J. Palmer, to a sophisticated worldwide movement. Chiropractors, nutritionists, physical therapists, Rolfers, Touch for Health body workers, yoga instructors—the list is long—have all advanced this broad approach to human well-being. Techniques such as detoxification of the body, brain-hemisphere balancing, nutritional balancing, the releasing of energy blockages in the chakras, creative visualization, and affirmations are all being continually refined and diffused into wider segments of the world's population. They work, as millions of people can now attest.

Sweetest of all the health-care advances being made is the worldwide growth in spiritual awareness that is turning multitudes of lives around. This is the Force that will change the world's mass thoughtforms, transmuting them into energies on higher, lighter vibration levels. As a result of this Force, even death is losing its sting, and we are waking up to the reality of our cosmic connections and potentials. What chance does the Grim Reaper projection (or the Satan projection, for that matter) have against the manifestations outpouring from Elisabeth Kübler-Ross and veteran psychic investigator Herald Sherman and Jane Roberts and all the unsung heroes of this spiritual tide? The human race is growing its own guardians.

As long as humans are involved in incarnations on the physical plane, there will be matters of health and dis-ease to be addressed. But, from almost all the signs, things will be looking up. As the influences of dis-ease and dysphoria lessen in the world, it will be possible to focus our attention on brighter things. The idea that illness and ill feelings are the inevitable lot of humanity will perhaps be seen as the aberrant and unnecessary thoughtform that it is.

Chapter 20

EDUCATION

At first glance, education might seem like a prosaic subject for a book on future lives. But here, too, we find massive historical tides that have hardly been assessed and that will play their part in the upcoming spiral. For the first time ever in history, a large percentage of the entire Earth population is becoming somewhat educated. Never mind the quality of this education, which varies and fluctuates greatly—most important is the sheer quantity of it. This will eventually lead to a new qualitative level.

The idea of mass education is itself relatively new, historically speaking. The massive implementation of this idea is even newer. Until very recently, for example, it was generally asserted by many "authorities" that higher education was mostly wasted on women, blacks, and the lower classes—it was like "casting pearls before swine."

A few facts will demonstrate how this has been changing. In the United States in 1870, only 2 percent of the population finished high school; in 1910, only about 12 percent of the population finished high school; by 1990, this figure reached 75 percent. In 1910, less than 3 percent of the population finished college; today the figure is around 20 percent. The increases are comparable (even if the percentages are not as high) in most other countries of the world.

Anyone who has been around the arena of education will admit that we have some real troubles in this area in our transition times. In *The Aquarian Conspiracy*, Marilyn Ferguson asserts that education is the most fossilized and least transformed of our major social institutions, and I heartily agree. However, during most of our world's history, almost all people lived and died as uneducated illiterates with *no* formal education. They had "common sense" and intuition and knew how to do their tasks of farming or fishing or whatever. But they knew little or nothing about the high culture or the high civilization of their own countries. They participated only as laborers and cannon fodder and breeders in the "great events" recorded in our history books. Even a century ago, the idea of free public education for everyone was a radical, socialistic, and heretical notion, loudly condemned by conservatives as wasteful and dangerous.

Today, the ideal that is being pushed worldwide is that all members of society need to be educated. This is happening in developing Third World nations as well as in the industrialized ones, but it is not just a matter of idealism, by any means. Developing nations, whatever their political persuasions or forms of government, are discovering a cold fact of life in the modern world. They are finding that *they need an educated populace to join the world community*. They have found that they must educate in order to industrialize. Otherwise they just don't make it, and they watch other countries doing better than they are. This process transcends any politics, sooner or later, and the countries' leaders start pouring resources into mass education. In a brilliant study, the social researcher Jacques Delacroix found that the single factor most highly correlated with standard of living in the countries of the world was level of education.

In opening up mass education, all countries have had to struggle with a fundamental dilemma that might be called "programming versus enlightenment." Educators, and especially those who pay and control them, want their pupils to develop "right thinking" that aligns them with their society's values, moral positions, and prevailing collective thought-forms. Communists and capitalists and religious fanatics alike want their citizens to manifest accepted values and standards. As anthropologist Jules Henry noted, this is part of the "hidden curriculum" of *every* formal schooling program in the world.

Simultaneously, however, those in control want a populace educated to reason logically and scientifically, and they want students to gain the necessary technical knowledge to perform complex jobs. But how can you train someone to be logical until five o'clock and then be ideological in their unquestioning beliefs? No one has really resolved this dilemma (thank God!). Part of the problem is that knowledge eventually blows away rhetoric and public relations. The recent "thaw" occurring in many Eastern bloc countries, for instance, has resulted partly from the fact that larger numbers of people in these countries are learning how much better off and more productive many Western nations are. China recently faced this dilemma squarely because of the massive student protests and popular cry for democratization. The old-guard government chose ruthless repression, to everyone's loss, and is now slowly learning that it didn't work.

Countries simply cannot keep the lid on this kind of data anymore in our global village. They *do* need trained professionals. So enlightenment is slowly winning out. It is getting harder and harder for leaders to keep their populations entirely uninformed and provincial. Indeed, it looks like the upcoming historical spiral will see the virtual end of this sort of provincialism, in which people know only what their leaders want them to.

For many people, education has been a very personal triumph. Tens of millions of people have achieved upward mobility and a better life situation through education. In America, this has been the main avenue "up and out" for millions of women, blacks, American Indians, and those born into the lower classes. In our transition times there is still educational discrimination, although its mechanisms are subtle. For example, in the United States in 1990, about one-quarter of the white population had completed college, but only about one-eighth of the black population, and only about one-sixteenth of Native Americans. Certainly, we have not reached educational equality, but these figures are an awesome improvement from what they were even half a century ago. There has also been an explosive growth in adult education. In Europe, more than one-tenth of the entire adult population is engaged full time in either teaching or learning.

The world educational level is rising each decade. We have never had a world population educated before. We don't really know where it will lead.

Education is not the total panacea for uplifting populations that social reformers once thought it might be. There have been highly educated intellectuals aiding and abetting some of the most heinous tyrants and wretched causes of modern times Education, which is a mental activity, must be balanced with activation of the chakras related to the physical, emotional, and spiritual planes. It was mentioned earlier that one of the Eastern mystics, Sri Swami Rama, noted that if you want to strive for enlightenment, your mind will help you; and if you want to commit murder, your mind will help you too. We must have heart and spirit in the equation.

There is a lot of world education going on in addition to that which is taught in the public school and college systems. Television, newspapers, and magazines, despite their bad-news distortions, are also a window on the world for hundreds of millions of people. Hundreds of millions of nonfiction books are also sold each year throughout the world. Again, the quality varies tremendously, but the sheer *quantity* of these influences compared with any earlier spiral is the really important point.

There is a great grassroots educational program going on in the world today, almost entirely outside of official channels. Esoteric institutes, informal groups, and individuals are doing their best to educate the populace in the leading-edge developments of the human-potential movement. This is still very much a minority movement, spreading through word of mouth along the strands of personal networks. It involves a diffuse education in new paradigms—in mind shifts. Almost no conventional school system honors it, or even acknowledges its existence, yet in every large city there are now seminars and workshops each weekend on these leading-edge topics. They are part of the bridge to a new world.

Not all is well with conventional education. For one thing, *mass* education presents many problems: huge anonymous lecture halls and faceless hordes of students who receive little or no individual attention or guidance in their growth.

Also, there is a deep conservative bias in mainstream education. From this conservative vantage point, leading-edge material is regarded as disreputable. Schools often simply have old-world textbooks with new copyright dates. Despite the slick packaging, they are no more leading edge than your grandmother's faded photo albums.

The vast majority of public school textbooks are painstakingly left brained and as drab as summer dust. They are carefully edited to offend no one, and as a result they inspire no one either. No wonder disrespect is an epidemic problem in the schools.

Asking most people about their school days opens floodgates through which pour streams of resentment, bitterness, frustration, and grief. There has to be a better way. Mass education is certainly better than no education at all, but it is certainly not good enough for a new era.

There is also a good deal of repetitive ritualism in schools.

For instance, math students are still doing their problems by hand rather than with pocket calculators (which their instructors always privately use). Mass education is very ill equipped to further the flowering of creativity. It can be a tedious and endless one-third of a person's life span—and needlessly so. There is an almost psychotic obsession with test-score standings among the Japanese. There is an archaic tenure system in most schools that allows incompetents to remain on the job—a system that no private industry could afford. There is bureaucratic harassment and burnout and low pay for instructors, leading many of the best to leave. After many years of left-brain mental drudgery, the system often ends up with relatively indifferent and burned-out instructors facing rows of relatively indifferent and burned-out students.

Granting all of these points, however, education is still a "window on the world." As someone once said, "If you think education is difficult and expensive, try ignorance!" All of these troubles, real as they are, are only minor discordances in the major historical sweep toward an educated planet.

Education breeds further education; it "rubs off" through peripheral learning as a contagion or diffusion. We continually educate one another, so the more educated we are, the more we spread education. New techniques, such as the brain-hemispheric balancing with which the Monroe Institute is experimenting, and the direct recovery of past-life knowledge and skills through widespread regression techniques may soon transform education into something entirely different from what it has ever been before.

There is a peculiar thing about knowledge as a commodity: it is not limited. If I have a dollar and I give it to you, I have a dollar less, but if I know something and I teach it to you, we *both* now have the knowledge. So knowledge, unlike dollars, has the potential for infinite expansion. A moment's reflection might reveal that this "expandable" characteristic of knowledge has many practical and mystical implications.

Leaving everything else aside, the main problem with current mass education is that it perpetuates prevailing mass thoughtforms to some extent. To some degree, education and mass communications work to preserve the old order by widely disseminating old images.

A little over a century ago, educators told us that human flight was impossible because the body would shatter under high speeds. A few decades later they told us we couldn't fly faster than the speed of sound. Shortly thereafter they proved to us with elegant mathematics that it was impossible to achieve escape velocity from the Earth's gravitational field, so spaceflight was out of the question. Now our textbooks tell us that the speed of light is an impossible barrier to cross, so real interstellar flight is impossible. And so it will be. . .until somebody does it.

Most human-potential therapists have remarked that they never learned what they needed during their conventional academic training. One way or another, they had to go beyond their schooling, outside of conventional channels, to gain the skills they needed.

Many people are coming to realize the difference between learning and schooling. They get their education wherever they can find it. From a more vaulting perspective, the whole world is our schoolroom on our individual and collective evolutionary journeys. And dozens of different mystical traditions affirm that the soul remembers.

At the risk of being utterly heretical. . .

One might learn more by studying Louise Hay's *You Can Heal Your Life* than by studying Freud and Jung or an introductory psychology text.

One might get more from studying Matthew Fox's *Original Blessing* than from studying Thomas Aquinas.

One might understand more from studying Peter Russell's *The Global Brain* or Willis Harman's *Global Mind Change* than from studying Darwin.

One might receive more enlightenment from studying Chelsea Quinn Yarbro's *Messages From Michael* or Jane Roberts's *Seth Speaks* than from pondering the *I Ching* or *The Upanishads.*

One might do better to read Teilhard de Chardin's works than those of either Plato or Aristotle.

Not surprisingly, seminal works are often "unconventional" and "disreputable" in their own times.

Chapter 21

ECONOMICS

Here's an irony. The majority of people find the subject of economics exceedingly dull and erudite, yet these people are vitally concerned, if not obsessed, with their own personal economic situations. The verb form of the word "economics" gives us a clue to our problems in this area. To "economize" means to manage and guard scarce resources; it implies scarcity. This concept, as a mass thoughtform echoing from earlier historical spirals, is a distortion that now gravely misleads our thinking on the topic of economics. It must be changed.

A huge mental shift occurs when we begin to think of economics as the study of *abundances* and their uses. We have been programmed to think of scarcities and their management when the facts are really otherwise. We hear of water shortages when six-sevenths of the globe is covered with water. The image of an energy shortage is simply collective madness in a universe awash and brimming over with all kinds of energies. And then there are food shortages. . .yet we pay farmers *not* to produce. A fourth of the world's population is dieting while another fourth is hungry. Almost all professionals agree that, except for political and economic barriers, we could easily keep all the peoples of the world well fed. Millions of people compulsively hoard and overeat and consume because they did without and faced so many threats of scarcity while living in previous spirals. But look around and you can see that we inhabit a vegetation-overgrown, water-rich, energy-soaked world. All the necessary *potentials* are here with us.

It is not useful to dwell on scarcities. It is important instead to think of harvesting our abundances. If we spent on the research a tiny fraction of what we now spend on military budgets, we could easily come up with the necessary process to convert sea water into usable domestic water, and we could develop cheap, safe alternative energy sources, such as large-storage-capacity solar batteries.

Economies have to do with the production, distribution, and consumption of goods and services, and "economics" is the study of these things; however, conventional economics is shot through with old-world images and fixed ideas about the cosmos. Also, it concentrates on the two upper, most superficial levels of social change and mostly misses the deeper tidal level of change, so it is not really very useful as it is ordinarily taught. There is a sour joke among inside investors: If 70 percent of the leading economists forecast something, plan on the opposite.

How goods and services are (1) produced, (2) distributed, and (3) consumed is almost unrecognizably different within different historical spirals. Each new spiral has involved a tremendous expansion of all three factors. For example, in late Industrial Spiral societies, over three-fourths of the labor force is engaged in jobs that didn't even exist a few centuries ago. Over the last century in the United States, there has been a steady shift of the majority of workers from the primary sector (agriculture and mining) to the secondary sector (manufacturing and refining) to the tertiary sector (service and information processing). Farming and industry are now carried on more efficiently by a smaller fraction of the total work force, and yet the varieties of goods and services now available to the

majority of people would be beyond belief to someone living
even a century ago. The modern supermarket, discount
department store, and shopping mall are, historically speaking, *wonderlands*.

There has also been an explosion of international trade in
our transition times. Just in the last thirty years, the United
States, for instance, has gone from importing less than one-
tenth of its total goods to importing well over one-fifth. The
massive increase in international commerce has made the
nations of the world far more interdependent, financially and
economically, than ever before in history. We are still learning
how to manage and live with this new situation of mutual
dependency. In addition, growth in the international exchange
of information and technologies is even more spectacular. So if
you are unsure about what is going on in these areas, don't feel
alone. Our experts and leaders aren't too sure either.

There are lots of other economic changes in our transition
times that portend our future lives. One of the most important is the steady rise in the amount of leisure time available
to the average person in modern societies. The visionary British economist Ralf Dahrendorf estimates that the average
work week in modern societies has been cut in half during the
last century (counting shorter hours, paid vacations, and legal
holidays). He points out that as people work less and less the
"labor society" is disappearing. This means the fading of
labor as a major life preoccupation. The subsequent rise of leisure in our time is not just for the privileged few, as it was in
earlier historical spirals, but for a large proportion of other
class members as well. The importance of this increased leisure time cannot be overestimated—leisure has always been a
requisite for the further development of civilization. Widespread leisure time acts as a springboard for the next spiral
because it allows very large numbers of people to have the
time and resources to invest in its birthing. In fact, such wide-

spread leisure is probably a necessary precondition for the onset of the new era.

A non-labor-oriented society might be something of a vacuum today, because many people carry strong past programming about having to work hard in order to be decent people. They may hold archaic notions such as "Idle hands are the devil's workshop." However, some adjustments are already starting to occur in our transition times. People don't as strongly identify themselves and each other by their jobs. There is a mushrooming of nonwork activities and personal pursuits. This is a real change from even the recent past.

For someone with a freer mind and spirit, there are endless things to do. For a more awake and aware society, there are endless projects as well. It's fun to try to imagine what they might be.

Economies have harbored a polarity that has haunted us all for some time and that we are finally beginning to transcend: the polarity of capitalism versus communism / socialism. The fact that we think of these ideologies as opposing gives us a clue to some of the distortions involved in our perception of them, similar to our exaggeration and false opposition of individual interests *versus* collective interests. Both poles are, of course, important. The silliness of our either / or perceptions has caused untold, unnecessary miseries and has prematurely terminated a good many incarnations.

The extreme of individualism, epitomized by unbridled capitalism, was based on the idea that if everyone just pursued their own self-interest this would somehow automatically be in the best interest of all. The extreme collectivism polarity, epitomized by unbridled communism, was based on the idea that if everything belonged to the state, and was collectively owned by the workers, an earthly paradise would follow. In their heydays, both were justified by lofty ideologies but had to be backed up with the force of their states to hang together. A false dilemma of liberty versus equality was posed, and a

great deal of propaganda was bandied about. Such lofty propaganda often covered utterly ruthless activities carried out
"beneath the veil" by both concerned parties. The fact is,
either extreme has proven to be entirely unworkable in a modern post-industrial society.

Most modern societies have been led through evolutionary forces to adopt what is called a "mixed economy"—one
that blends aspects of both capitalism and socialism. This
type of economy entails higher living standards for the successful strivers (and their heirs), combined with some guaranteed level of subsistance and services for all. This solution and
integration is arrived at in nation after nation, whatever their
original political ideologies or cultural roots, because it seems
to best fit the conditions of our transition times. This is
another sign of the integration of the gross imbalances of
earlier historical spirals. The realistic promise is that *everyone
can be more prosperous.*

In our transition times, there are troubling situations
related to our economies. One of these situations is that the
fact of our continually growing worldwide economic interdependence has outstripped our *awareness* of it. Beneath our
regional and international economic conflicts and competi-
tions is a thickening web of interconnectedness that few
leaders and decision-makers seem to really grasp. The interlocking debts and trade deficits and floating currencies
among nations are something of a house of cards, held
together by continuous negotiations and interventions. We
are, collectively, still in the process of learning how to live an
interdependent life. It may be scary to realize that the only
real value of the dollar bill in one's pocket is its exchange rate
against five other currencies, but this is the new way of the
world.

Another problem is the dislocations in individual lives, in
organizations, and even in geographic regions that happen as
widespread economic shifts continue to occur. Families and

whole regions experience booms and busts as the transition to a new spiral unfolds. This is causing subtle attitude shifts in which people and organizations are taking the orderly stability of "reality" less for granted. It is also swelling adult education in all modern countries. It is becoming far more common now for people to have more than one career during a single lifetime. However, many individuals suffer personally from these dislocations. For example, economic convulsions have swelled the ranks of the homeless, both here and in most Third World countries. This is why a safety net of guaranteed subsistence services becomes so important. Such a safety net will almost certainly be part of our next historical spiral; rudimentary forms of it already exist in some European countries.

Another troubling situation, brand new in history, is the rise of giant multinational corporations in our time. Each of these giant conglomerates may deal in everything from mining copper to making movies to manufacturing jet fighters and baby food to creating medical drugs to publishing newspapers to bottling your favorite soft drink. Some of them operate in fifty or more different countries, and their yearly gross receipts exceed the gross national product of most members of the United Nations. They are not necessarily malignant, but their philosophy rests on such things as quarterly profit statements and percent of market share. In pursuit of their goals, they greatly influence events, often accidentally and unintentionally, because of their sheer size. For instance, a "minor" board-meeting decision by one of these corporations can make or break the economy of a small Third World country or cause a depression and the collapse of real estate prices in a small American city (as portrayed in the recent movie *Roger and Me*). This is the old story of the giant accidentally stepping on the pygmy. These corporations wield enormous, behind-the-scenes political power, and there are few checks and balances on their actions. A certain degree of ruthlessness and tunnel vision is inherent in their operations.

In a somewhat similar vein, several top-ranking professions have become highly organized, monopolistic, and very powerful in their political and economic influence. Doctors, lawyers, and real estate brokers and developers, acting as special-interest groups, have succeeded in getting laws passed that are very favorable to themselves but very questionable for consumers and the environment. Doctors and lawyers, especially, have also managed to gain almost complete control over the standards and ethics within their own professions—a situation that leads to self-protection far more than it does to self-policing, according to most critics. Every working professional knows individuals within his or her own field who are utterly incompetent, if not outright fraudulent. However, for the sake of protecting the profession, real action is seldom taken against them.

Operating more out of self-interest than collective interest, many corporations and professions have been criminally abusive toward the Earth's environment. This trend has been continuing throughout the Industrial Spiral. For instance, London has been frequently blanketed by hazardous smog from coal burning in homes and industries. In our own time, the cumulative abuses have reached the point of potential ecocide. Witness the 1989 Exxon *Valdez* oil-spill disaster. Happily, the world seems to be slowly waking up to this fact.

The multinationals and the organized professions raise serious ethical questions that have definitely not yet been resolved. The deeper ethical question is, however, To what extent are we as humans one another's economic keepers? Our gross imbalances have cut off our perceptions to the point that we might erroneously let this question slide, perhaps giving a bit of money for the needy during the holidays or tossing some coins into a canister for hungry overseas children. This will no longer do, for both practical and deeply spiritual reasons.

We are all interconnected. To some degree, we all go together into the next spiral and we all share our future lives. Whatever we turn our backs on today is likely to eventually grab us from behind.

We can do it. We can provide for ourselves and all our fellow human beings. The potentials of automation and robotics and the technologies of abundance are probably beyond our wildest current imaginings, but these potentials are already within our grasp. There are some who say these things can't be done, but what do they know? There have always been people in a given historical spiral who have denied the possibilities of those things that prevail in the following spiral. We must show them by providing for them, too.

The visionary psychologist Abraham Maslow set forth a hierarchy of human needs ranging from immediate survival to vaulting spirituality. If we can handle the lower levels of this hierarchy for the human race—providing subsistence and a modicum of security and comfort—then humans can concentrate on the higher levels of human needs. At that point we will, in truth, experience an astonishing new era in our future lives.

Chapter 22

ENVIRONMENT

A few years ago, when I began telling audiences that environmental issues would become the most talked about pressing problems of the nineties and beyond, I was met with stony silence. ("What the hell is he talking about?") A couple years later, my remarks were met with derogatory denials. ("Oh come on, don't exaggerate.") Soon thereafter, my comments evoked a kind of hysterical rejection response, probably due to a dawning awareness of what I was implying. ("Yah, yah, I don't want to hear it.") Today, I'm getting excited comments and emotional debates. ("What can we do?") Now the facts are beginning to pile up, and they add up to ominous scenerios:

Scientists have found toxins and pollutants even in the cells of creatures inhabiting such remote regions as Greenland and Antarctica.

Current government reports indicate that over half of the American population is living in areas that have dangerous air-quality levels.

Massive worldwide deforestation and the continued burning of fossil fuels have measurably increased the percentage of carbon dioxide and other contaminants in the Earth's atmosphere.

The acidity of rain in the northeastern United States, eastern Canada, and other regions has increased thirtyfold during the last few decades.

Every day, several species of plants and animals become extinct.

The ozone layer, which protects the surface of the planet from dangerous radiation levels, is being depleted, and several holes in it have been charted.

The Greenhouse Effect—the warming of the Earth, which was considered a weird, science fiction notion only a few years ago—is now with us for real.

Carl Sagan, the internationally renowned scientist, and his associates have calculated that even a "minor" nuclear battle would result in a "Nuclear Winter." The debris thrown into the upper atmosphere would create a worldwide sooty shroud that would drastically reduce the surface temperature of the planet long enough for most of humanity to freeze or starve to death. Scientist Stephen Schneider points out that, in such a nuclear battle, the attacker would "win" for only about two weeks.

We have rapidly growing mountains of toxic wastes and nowhere safe to put them. They are contaminating the waters of the planet.

The trees are dying.

The list could go on and on.

These facts are important, to be sure, but even more important for our future is the degree of awareness people have of such facts.

With regard to the environment, humanity's major imbalances and barriers are running rampant. It is easy to see some of their insidious results. We have manifested an extreme degree of aggressiveness and little or no caregiving in our treatment of the biosphere and of other life-forms. There are rampant self-interests and vested interests in the actions of corporations and land developers, coupled with an abysmal neglect of humanity's collective interests. Mechanistic Newtonian thinking and materialism have led to the treatment of the environment and the creatures within it as *things,* with no sensitivity toward their living spiritual qualities. Old norms and fixed ideas have engendered rapacious attitudes in which our ecology is perceived as an inexhaustible treasure house to be despoiled for profit and convenience. Additionally, future shock has produced a numb disbelief that the environmental crisis even exists.

We are talking about our own living quarters. During the time we inhabit the physical plane, we remain alive only through the supporting embrace of the environment. There is a fundamental, inescapable, continuous interaction between our surroundings and ourselves. If you hold your breath for just one minute, this point will come home.

We collectively create the environment we inhabit. Real-estate friends have shown me several houses that have been thoroughly trashed by their tenants, and it is a sobering experience. Half-decayed refuse is piled about in every corner. There are holes in the walls, broken doors and windows, dried feces in the closet, grease filming everything, unidentifiable stains on the floors, torn carpets, and a pervasive smell of rot and urine. It takes a great deal of work and thousands of dollars to rehabilitate such a house to the point where it can be a place of gracious living again. On a far larger scale, this is what humanity has been doing with the planet. If you think of Earth as our mother, you might say that we have taken brass knuckles to our mother's face.

Ironically, it is self-interest that is waking some people up to our environmental problems. Early incidents, such as the poisoning of Love Canal and the Three Mile Island nuclear-plant disaster, stirred only mild ripples of concern for personal safety, except among those immediately involved. However, the continuing string of ecological incidents such as the

Chernobyl nuclear meltdown in Russia, the Alaskan oil spill, bizarre droughts, storms, heat waves, and the mounting number of toxic spills have finally begun to reach more people's awareness. Visions of coughing for the rest of their lives or seeing malignant blooms in the x-rays of their bodies are beginning to haunt people and bring home the environmental truths.

There are ironies upon ironies in the environmental crisis. At the same time that we are facing unprecedented environmental menaces, our environmental control and comforts are at an all-time high. We can do more *with* and *to* our environment than ever before. Living in many parts of the world would be almost intolerable without modern heating and air conditioning, for example. The hot shower has increased longevity, as mentioned previously. Our stores are stocked with items from distant parts of the world. Electricity has extended our abilities in a thousand different ways. We are designing artificial environments for living in space.

The human race is currently experiencing a technological double-edged sword. Our technology is providing us with the basis for better living and also for reaching higher evolutionary spirals, but at the same time it is creating the environmental menaces we are now facing. The environmental problems are very real, but technology is also our only way out. Technology is both the culprit and the savior. Fortunately, as Carl Sagan is fond of saying, we are very good at figuring things out. A great many people have pointed out that it is not technology itself but *our use of it* that will determine what our future lives will be like.

I am not a trained ecologist, but I am a trained research evaluator. In looking over a sample of the emerging environmental reports, I have noticed two basic troublemaking processes at work.

First, there is the multitudinous pollution of our planet—the air, the water, and the land. Each of these many pollution situations deserves a book by itself. Just as a sufficient amount of toxin can overwhelm a human body, the pollution of the Earth threatens to overwhelm its planetary life-support systems. It has already been irrefutably documented that this pollution has killed off much planetary life, from lichens and sea creatures to trees. European environmentalists have termed this "the green death." In addition to it being a nitty-gritty issue about survival, this wholesale extinction of myriad life-forms cannot help but have some spiritual implications.

The second major category of environmental problems is the upsetting of the dynamic processes that ordinarily balance the Earth's biosphere, maintaining homeostasis so that the world remains hospitable to life. These include weather-exchange systems, which damp out any local excesses; heat and radiation exchange systems between the planet's surface and outer space; systems that maintain and adjust the optimum mixture of gases in the atmosphere; water circulation systems; and stress-balancing systems for the Earth's crust. Through the eons, these homeostatic processes have displayed an ability to handle and re-balance fairly extreme fluctuations, but currently we are stretching a bit far Mother Earth's ability to heal herself. Also, *the more out of whack the misalignments become, the more convulsive the adjustments will need to be.* This is a dangerous collective gamble.

If there were no spiritual basis for life, I suppose one might say, What the hell, let the future take care of the future. However, as surveyed in my recent book, *The Emerging New Age,* there is now massive evidence for the spiritual basis of life. Also, aside from its callous brutality, a "to hell with the future" perspective misses the point that many of these ecological consequences are already with us. And more of them will be upon us in a matter of years, not decades or centuries. We have troubles now and troubles down the road.

Ecologists assure us that many of the technical problems arising in the environment are not too difficult to resolve. It is our low collective awareness of them that allows these problems to continue and worsen. What we must deal with are our own imbalances and barriers—exemplified by inertia, ruthless special interests, and tribal politics—in the face of global concerns (just as we must deal with fierce sectarian religions in the face of global spiritual concerns).

There is an easily documented fact about the environment that might be startling to many people. Almost all multinational corporations and national governments have, by their actions, proven to be unfriendly toward the planet. These groups offer much window dressing, many calls for conferences, and endless streams of public relations, but behind the blue smoke and mirrors, pretty much the same old deals go down. Environmentalism is not a movement by corporations and governments; it is a grassroots people's movement.

Carl Sagan has suggested that people should vote only for candidates with proven environmental records, being sure to look beyond the rhetoric of their speech writers. This might help, but the ability of politicians to manipulate their public images has, so far, proven mostly effective against this ploy. Additionally, most of the media have gone along with and abetted such manipulations. (There is extensive coverage of political news conferences and committee reports that usually end up going nowhere.)

A more fundamental solution seems to be inherent in our progressive uplifting into the next evolutionary spiral. It can be observed by most anyone and runs like this. Unaware people tend to harm the environment a great deal and help it little if at all. More aware people tend to harm the environment much less and to help and nurture it much more. From these two crucial facts it can be deduced that as collective awareness continues to rise, environmental excesses will lessen and multitudes of healing actions will be taken. Even in our own times, devastated inner-city districts have often been restored to beauty and usefulness, so we know that revitalization can occur. People's self-interest can also be harnessed through education about the facts of environmental life.

Incidently, I know that Carl Sagan has not been too friendly toward most of the human-potential movement. He has, for example, sometimes gone out of his way to make highly critical statements about psychic healing, paranormal phenomena, and astrology. However, he has been a steadfast, outspoken opponent of maniacal government policies toward the environment, long before it was the "in" thing to do. He stepped forward to brand the "Star Wars" Strategic Defense Initiative a transparent hoax while most of the Western world just rolled over and smiled. He has been jailed for protesting nuclear-weapons tests. He made the initial calculations and discovered the phenomenon of "nuclear winter," much to the dismay of the arms racers. And he has gambled a shining career for the sake of his love of the planet and for the dream of getting humanity into space. I await the day when he is more open toward things spiritual, but that is his choice and his journey.

I am bringing up Sagan's case because it emphasizes a very important point. The intermittent feuding between Sagan and some New Agers might obscure the far more important fact that both parties are actively midwifing the birth of a higher evolutionary spiral. The feuds will be forgotten in future histories, but the good works of each camp will not.

There is both hard science and high mysticism regarding our planet. The mystical traditions of many peoples have perceived the environment as a living configuration, within which humans are nestled. This perceived aliveness includes not only the plants and animals; it includes the hills and rivers, the winds and the seasons, and the planet itself.

For a time, modern people dismissed such a notion as "animism," an aspect of primitive superstition. However, in our transition times there is growing to be a wondrous merger between science and mysticism with respect to the environment. This blending is manifested, for example, in the works of the maverick genius Buckminster Fuller and in the dogged efforts of Greenpeace and the Sierra Club to save the environment. It has become even more explicit in the work of internationally acclaimed scientist James Lovelock and his successors. Using the latest hard-science data, Lovelock startled the scientific community by formulating the "Gaia Hypothesis." This hypothesis states that Gaia, or Mother Earth, displays the characteristics of a *living system.*

In *The Global Brain*, British visionary physicist Peter Russell discusses how Earth displays both self-regulating and self-organizing properties. "Gaia appears to be a self-regulating, self-sustaining system, continually adjusting its chemical, physical, and biological processes in order to support life and its continuing evolution." Russell shows that our planet displays all of the nineteen characteristics of living systems established in the new science General Systems Theory. *Gaia, the Earth Mother, is a living system in her own right.*

The scientific, ethical, and spiritual implications of this hypothesis are simply awesome. An explanation of it, according to one line of reasoning, is that all matter naturally and inherently evolves higher and higher levels of consciousness. According to another line of reasoning, all matter is a "solid" manifestation *of* consciousness. Whatever the ultimate truth is, one thing is certain. We are messing around with some deep and powerful cosmic forces when we deal with the environment.

Russell and many others have suggested the further possibility that humanity and the environment are continuously evolving together in an intimate partnership. If this is indeed the case—that essentially *everything* in the universe is evolving together—then the outcome of this for our future lives is flatly unguessable. The idea that sentience is a natural characteristic of all things, great and small, may be as mysterious to many people as the vast and mysterious workings of the human body may be to a single cell within it.

The self-regulating and self-organizing aspects of Mother Earth as explained by the Gaia Hypothesis bring us the good news that we need If we just stop poisoning the Earth Mother, she will heal herself. And then, even from her own sickbed, she will bring *us* the flowers.

Chapter 23

POLITICS

In our transition times, one of the areas that many people are the most disheartened about is politics. In these people's minds, politics has become a dirty word, and they see political abuses and the rule of special interests as the order of the day throughout much of the world. Some people dive into the political arena with a kind of desperate bravura, hoping to reform some aspect of the social structure by joining an action group. Others develop a permanent sneer toward the subject and will have nothing to do with it. In many parts of the world, people risk their lives on a daily basis by striving to better things through political strife. Meanwhile, all of us are ruled rather badly most of the time.

It has been worse. The kings and conquerors and despotic lordlings of earlier historical spirals were far more arbitrary in their rule than most modern governments are able to be. Hitler did not invent genocide, nor did Stalin invent slaughtering whole segments of his own country's population. In earlier times, politics was almost entirely an autocratic rule by force of a relative handful of men from the privileged groups who were backed up by rigid traditions and abetting religions. Even in the founding days of the United States, only about 30 percent of the adult population had the right to vote.

There have been lofty philosophical definitions of politics—such as "the art of ruling"—but, unfortunately, these definitions usually have had little to do with the raw realities of political history. In reality, politics has been most concerned with the distribution and manifestation of *power*, both within and between societies. This power can take many forms: legal, economic, traditional, forceful, charismatic, or by manipulation of collective images. The fact that politics has to do with power, dominance, and influence is the reason why so many individuals and groups are keenly interested in it.

Those in positions of political dominance make the rules, not only for themselves, but also for all the other people living in their society. Minorities are always underrepresented politically, yet minority members have to live under the laws and administrations of more privileged groups. If minority people's ways of life differ significantly from that of the groups in power, they are in a sense living under a "foreign domination." For example, as mentioned previously, one-half of the United States population is female and about one-eighth is black, but one-half of the United States senators and representatives have never been female, nor have one-eighth of them been black. Minority group members are also very scarce among the Fortune 500's top executives. Men make most of the laws women must live by, and whites make most of the rules for blacks.

Those in political power have also been in positions to heavily influence a society's major institutions—its education systems, religious organizations, commerce, and justice systems. These institutions therefore tend to reflect the belief structures and special interests of the prevailing powerful groups. The rest of the populace is then heavily programmed and propagandized about the rightness of "the way things are," based on the belief systems of these prevailing groups. This has tended to perpetuate mass thoughtforms such as "my country right or wrong," which were so prevalent during earlier times.

The predominance of the self-interest pole over the collective-interest pole shows up clearly in the political arena. Historically, politics has been strewn with examples of short-sighted self-interest, such as the disastrous failure of the nobility to grant concessions to commoners in previous times, leading to unnecessary, bloody revolutions. The violence of the French, Russian, and Chinese revolutions could probably have been avoided if the privileged groups had accommodated some of the needs and desires of the rest of the populace. In an extensive study of political violence in many different countries, sociologist Edward Muller found that there were two factors particularly related to high violence levels: (1) great inequality in income distribution and (2) great repressiveness of a regime. When these two factors are known and handled, bloody revolutions can be averted. This is a good thing to remember for the future: negotiated accommodation works and defuses violence.

The self-interest pole combined with the barrier of tribalism creates all kinds of mischief in the political relationships between nations. The underlying effect is a widespread failure to clearly perceive and understand one another on an international basis. In this vacuum of understanding, nations project dark collective thoughtforms upon one another. All through the Cold War, Americans perceived Russians as sinister revolutionaries and Russians perceived Americans as ruthless imperialists, so true dialogue was difficult and the two groups' many common interests and interconnections were overshadowed. The failure of the United States to comprehend South American and Middle East politics is another example. The consequences of these misunderstandings are frequently unintended—for instance, U.S. intervention in Vietnam and El Salvador, and Russia's presence in Afghanistan and its own ethnic minority regions. Often, the end result of such meddlings is only the laying waste of a country-side. Because of such ignorance, international politics have been little more than intrigues and misadventures.

The character of politics in different historical spirals can be seen today by comparing those modern countries in a late industrial phase with those just coming into the Industrial Spiral and those still having an agricultural focus. In almost all fully industrialized nations, politics, for all its intrigues and inequalities, is "softball"—orderly and more equitable than in earlier times. In agricultural and newly industrialized societies, politics is something of a walk on the wild side, consisting of autocracies, gross inequalities, state-sanctioned atrocities, and violent group conflicts. In these countries, politics is a very hazardous occupation.

It is becoming clear that violent revolutions don't work very well because, in reacting to a corrupt and inhumane regime, the revolutionaries are trapped into becoming corrupt and inhumane, too. The bulk of the French and Russian people were certainly worse off immediately following their respective revolutions. Political enlightenment must mean not replacing an old ideology with a new one, but outgrowing and transcending ideology as it has been understood. All the signs suggest that the "ideology" of the upcoming era will partly consist of a growing recognition of the companionship of all life forms. Such a recognition is bound to create massive changes in the political arena.

Politics is usually presented as a very complex subject, but it has an utterly simple bottom line. As long as humanity has a low collective awareness level and operates along the coarser-vibration wavelengths, people end up choosing, or at least accepting, political leaders who mirror this low level. And we don't just elect or allow individual leaders—we also get their whole network of cronies and collaborators, as recent scandals have shown. As an extreme example, Hitler reflected and reso-nated with not only a mass thoughtform of Germany at that time, but also a mass thoughtform of much of the Western world: white supremacy, fascist elitism, colonialism, "the white man's burden," ethnic bigotry, and so on. The world then suffered not only him, but also his political, military, and industrial buddies. In representative societies, all candidates reflect and resonate with prevailing thoughtforms to a great degree—or they would never be candidates. *Therefore, as we change our collective consciousness levels, the candidates will change.*

There is one very heartening trend in politics. Over the last century, most areas of the globe have become increasingly democratic. For example, all of Western Europe, Japan, India, and many former communist bloc nations now have far more democratic forms of government than in the recent past. No country is totally democratic, but the historical trend toward democracy is overwhelming. Democratization, incomplete as it always is, seems to be another of our major historical tides.

Throughout history, humans have longed for wise and good rulers, but they have very seldom gotten them. Some rulers have been ruinous, but mostly there have been mediocre ones who were distillations of people's immaturities and imbalances as spiritual beings. Politics has usually been the worst when the leaders have been zealots or egomaniacs. However, people have also usually suffered the most when they were personally in the grip of zealousness or egomania in their own lives, so this correspondence is no accident.

In our transition times, there are heartening signs. In most industrial countries, there has been a lessening of social distance between the leaders and the citizens. The "sacred" aspects of leadership have been fading, partly due to mass media coverage of leaders' lives and partly because of the growth in egalitarian ideals. As one example of this trend, all citizens in a democratic society, be they president or pauper, are ideally subject to the same laws. This is seldom entirely the case in practice, but as an ideal it has become a growing mass thoughtform.

In all modern societies, whatever their political persuasion, there is also the fact that a larger proportion of the populace is now sharing in political and administrative decisions. This is so for the very pragmatic and necessary reason that modern governments have become complex and interdependent with many other sectors of society, such as banking, commerce, and research. This means that more people share the power and that no handful of individuals can have it all. This is a lesson that dictator after dictator is slowly, and reluctantly, learning. Leaders *must* share decision making to have a country that runs at all. This is an odd, but very powerful, democratization process that shows every sign of increasing in the new spiral.

Another increasing form of "indirect democracy" is national opinion polls on a wide variety of issues. These are being gathered in the majority of countries now, and political leaders are becoming more and more sensitive to them as social barometers. *Competence* and some awareness of constituency opinions are becoming more and more important characteristics of leaders, whatever their stripes.

The world can still experience political "mad dogs" who stir up a lot of trouble and unrest, but even with these there is a promise of change. Through worldwide telecommunications and growing world interdependencies, there has been a growth in the "court of world opinion" that is becoming harder for any nation's leaders to ignore. For example, in the late 1980s Iran found itself virtually ostracized from the rest of the international community, including its Islamic neighbors. This created enough economic and other hardships to cause the Iranians to soften their rigid posture. Similar pressures influenced North Korea and North Vietnam (which won the war and lost the peace). At what point will a Hitler or Stalin just be laughed off the world stage?

So much of today's government is already brand new in history. All modern governments must engage in "social engineering" on a massive scale to keep their economies and other programs running. This involves everything from managing interest rates in consultation with other nations to negotiating world trade to administering international air traffic, waste disposal, and public health and welfare programs. Of necessity, our future lives may end up with government by *meritocracy*, that is, with leadership by ability.

According to Daniel Yankelovich's national opinion studies, in 1955, 55 percent of Americans agreed with the statement "Can trust the government to do what is right." By 1978, this figure had shrunk to 28 percent. As awareness rises, people become more independent and watchful. The visionary Luis Racionero said that the vision must be our own, or we shall remain slaves to the dreams of other men.

Chapter 24

WAR

The first thing to understand about war is this: A large number of scientists, spiritual leaders, and broken-hearted people have determined that war is extremely hazardous to our health.

War, including violent revolutions, seems to be the nastiest enterprise that humans engage in. It has intruded into every historical spiral so far. It has filled our history books and storybooks with famous names and dates—and pictures of widespread social and human wreckage.

"Why so much war?" people have asked from time immemorial. The answers to this question have been pretty strange. One answer has been that humans have an "aggressive instinct" because we are descended from "killer apes," so it is our nature to fight. However, anthropologists have found many societies that are not warlike. Several modern nations, such as Sweden and Switzerland, have sidestepped all wars for a long time now. As the eminent sociologist Ian Robertson has suggested, most people live peacefully most of the time and they are happy at the end of hostilities, so someone could just as easily argue that humans have a "peace-loving instinct."

Another response to the question is "the glory of war." The truth is that most soldiers are terrified of meeting the enemy, are often unsure about the reasons for fighting, and are not lovers of combat. It takes very intensive training to make youths into professional killers.

It is true that, historically, there have been warlike groups who have strongly socialized their young men in the ways of war. It is also true that military service has usually been a career for footloose youngsters and those down on their luck. (For example, the military currently provides job opportunities and upward social mobility for many disadvantaged American youths.) It is also true that the privileged classes have often demanded that their male members be skilled in the martial arts—for obvious reasons of self-preservation.

The immediate cause of most wars has been the result of actions taken by political leaders of the groups involved. The citizens have followed along, sometimes through necessity, as when they have been attacked or invaded. Often, though, citizens have been conscripted through a combination of duty, propaganda, and force. The results have been, more often than not, devastating, even for the "winners."

A deeper cause of war could be the unbalanced manifestation of male-polarity (yang) energies unchecked by an intermixing with female (yin) energies. Nowhere are the effects of an exaggerated dominance of male-principle energies so apparent as in war and other violent enterprises such as revolution and terrorism. In the common barbarous conditions of earlier historical spirals, such aggressive attributes may possibly have been useful, although their manifestation perpetuated the barbarity. Now these attributes are simply an unmitigated threat to humanity.

The millennia-long unbridled manifesting of such unbalanced energies has also set up some deep karmic habits and obsessions that need to be released and transcended. Today, many an upset person has been heard to say, "I could have killed them." Or, "I think he was about ready to kill me." These coarse-vibration-level responses are rampant in the world's populations. Got a problem? Kill someone!

The direct devastations of war itself are only the beginning of the costs of this unbalanced manifestation. It is estimated that the countries of the world, during the last quarter century, have spent fourteen trillion dollars (in mid-1980 currency value) on military items. The United States spends around twelve hundred dollars per capita per year on armaments. The economies of most nations are impoverished to a great degree by these expenditures, and they have been a main source of the staggering national debts of many nations, including the United States. According to sociologists Richard and Wendy Wallace, for every dollar the United States spends on domestic production, it spends thirty-three cents on the military. For every similar dollar of domestic production, West Germany spends thirteen cents on the military and Japan spends only two cents. This is one obvious reason why West Germany and Japan are in better financial shape than the United States.

Consider what could be done if just one-tenth of these funds were diverted into constructive purposes. There could be hundreds of thousands of college scholarships. The problem of the homeless could be easily handled. The United States could have a flourishing space-development program. As a lighthearted gesture, the U.S. government could buy every American citizen an ice cream cone. Wouldn't you rather have an ice cream cone than an M-16 bullet?

Violent group conflicts, whether foreign wars or internal civil wars and revolutions, produce convulsive changes in the lives of the hapless people involved and devastation of the environment. They are disruptive to all categories of human beings. Infants and children are traumatized on a mass basis and are often sacrificed one way or another. Young people have their life plans disrupted, often irrevocably. Adults see the niches they have established for themselves threatened and not infrequently destroyed. The elderly sometimes lack

the vigor to withstand the upheavals. Parents receive printed
notices from the government about their children's violent
deaths. Women and the homes and families they care for (in
both senses) are under threat of dissolution. Also, women easily become chattel and sexual receptacles. Privileged groups
sometimes fare better because of their greater resources, but
often not. The wealthy often become enriched during wars,
but during internal revolutions their lives hang in the balance. The majority of the nobility of France and Russia were
slaughtered during their revolutions. Tens of thousands of
landlords were massacred in the wake of the Chinese communist revolution. Where are the winners? At best, people
might learn some heavy lessons about what *not* to do and *not*
to allow in future lives.

*A great many scientists, spiritual leaders, and broken-
hearted people have determined that war is extremely hazardous to your health.*

There are ironies and dark humors around the subjects of
war, the arms race, and the "defense" industries. For example,
the United States and Russia have a tacit stalemate agreement
called MAD—Mutually Assured Destruction—through which
each country has the balanced ability to utterly waste the
other. Another example is the flight of Canadian geese mis-
identified as an incoming Russian attack, but correctly
reevaluated just in time to abort World War III. There are the
military toilet seats with four hundred dollar price tags that
any savvy shopper could find for under ten dollars. There is
the Bradley personnel carrier nicknamed "the Deathtrap"
and the nuclear submarine that, when launched in California,
promptly sank to the bottom of the ocean. There is the rampant fraud within the armaments industry: in the mid-1980s,
nine of the Pentagon's top ten contractors were under criminal
investigation, mostly for fraud and theft. During the last century, arms races and wars have been "good business" for many
of the world's largest multinational corporations.

Finally (not really) there is the Strategic Defense Initiative, "Star Wars," with an estimated price tag of one trillion dollars. If pushed through Congress, it promises to be the biggest boondoggle in human history. "Games" enthusiasts have already figured out a great many ways to foil it, even if it ever did become operational. For instance, any foreign agent with a nuclear-device-filled suitcase could utterly subvert it by destroying Washington, D.C., while Congress, the president, and the cabinet were in town.

All of the above are rather dismal thoughts. The crucial question is, Is there any hope? Happily, the answer is yes, there certainly is.

Some of the facts of our transition times are beginning to strongly mitigate against further wars, at least major ones. At the coarsest level, nations are, one by one, coming to realize that war is unprofitable and unpalatable. Americans in Vietnam, Russians in Afghanistan, Cubans in Angola, Iraqis, and Iranis slowly and painfully have learned that a country can win most of its battles and still lose a war. As social structures become more complex and populaces become more aware, it is becoming more and more difficult to militarily conquer a country and make it stick. It would be harder today for any leaders to get the United States into another Vietnam or Russia into another Afghanistan.

Even more important than this trend is the fact that all the things contributing to a worldwide rise in awareness and expectations are making war more unacceptable in the minds of Earth's population. Wars are probably harder to "sell" now than they have ever been. As the brilliant futurist Willis Harman says in his book *Global Mind Change*, wars are becoming increasingly "de-legitimized" in people's minds.

There's hope. One of the brightest signs is that polls around the world demonstrate that support for war is steadily declining. In Europe, there has been the recent rise of Green parties with environmental, anti-war political platforms. As another sign, 83 percent of a 1924 sample of U.S. midwestern students felt that "in the last war the United States was fighting in a wholly righteous cause." By 1977, in a similar sample, those responding this way had shrunk to 36 percent.

There was a saying in the sixties: "Someday they'll give a war and nobody will come." We might yet see this happen.

Chapter 25

CRIMINALITY

Crime is an ugly subject because, one way or another, it increases human misery. Crime is usually defined as a violation of the laws. There are crimes against persons and crimes against property; there are major crimes (felonies) and minor crimes (misdemeanors). In ordinary jurisprudence, a crime is something that violates the law as established by legitimate government authority. However, this definition will not do at all.

When criminality is looked at from higher perspectives, the view gets curiouser and curiouser. Several years ago in San Francisco, I idly watched a small boy park his bike and go into a store. As he came out with a candy bar, an older boy jumped onto his bike and raced away. The small boy collapsed on the sidewalk and began crying brokenheartedly. *Legally,* this crime was only a minor offense committed by a juvenile.

During the Second World War, a young German officer, a war hero, was sentenced to "hazardous duty" for protesting the mass executions of Jews. *Legally,* he had violated army regulations.

Several centuries ago, the British Crown commissioned a number of pirates to harass the Spaniards and pay 10 percent of their loot into the royal treasury. *Legally,* these "privateers" were serving the British government as they pillaged, raped, and slaughtered Spanish ships, lands, and people. (Meanwhile, the Spaniards were doing similar "legal" things to Native American tribes.)

In recent years, the United States Congress has kept many unnecessary military bases open and has allowed huge expenditures for experimental weapons systems that are the laughingstocks of experts and the bane of military field personnel. These appropriations have impoverished the average middle-class family by several hundred dollars a year in taxes, yet *legally*, the wishes of various special interests and congressional districts have been served. All sorts of special-interest groups are also *legally* trashing our ecosystems.

Criminality and breaking a law are therefore not really the same thing, so a better definition for criminality must be found elsewhere. Far too often, laws are at least partly the reflections of local moral customs, political expediency, and the vested interests of the groups with power over legislatures in that society.

A more vaulting and useful definition of criminality might be *the significant violation of human rights*. The greater the human rights violation, the more heinous the crime! Under this definition, anything that interferes with an individual's life, liberty, and pursuit of happiness would be criminal. A law based on this definition was offered in Frank Herbert's *Dune*: "Thou shalt not disfigure the human soul." An even more bold definition of criminality would be anything that grossly violates the Universal Declaration of Human Rights, signed in 1948 by all members of the United Nations and upheld by none of them. This document could actually serve quite nicely as a credo for the upcoming spiral. (It is reprinted in the Appendix.)

Enough theories about the causes of criminality, ranging from genetic to sociological, exist to make anyone's head swim. However, from a spiritual perspective the subject can be seen more clearly. There are two broad characteristics of almost all criminality:

1. A grave imbalance in the self-interest/collective-interest polarity, producing a bias toward self-interest, shortsightedness, and lack of empathy for others. Extended into us/them tribalism, this produces similar ills in both intergroup and international relations. "Anything goes" because it's "them." Those with an exaggerated self-interest pole cannot see the karmic consequences of their actions upon others—or even upon themselves in the long run. Under the influence of such spiritual blindness, criminality "makes sense" to them. They can't count the costs when they can't *see* the costs.

2. A strong presence of the coarser, darker energy wavelengths, causing psychic pollution and negativities. This negative energy presence also produces contagion; that is, those who are criminalized in turn tend to criminalize others. For example, many studies have shown that a large percentage of violent criminals were themselves victims of child abuse. (However, not all victims of abuse become criminals.) Crimes of passion, violence, and brutality can manifest only at low vibration levels, and they often result from unreleased violent patterns established during lives lived in earlier violent historical spirals.

Crimes that include emotions such as rage, resentment, viciousness, spite, and lust also resonate with the coarser energies. Less-evolved beings of the low astral planes simultaneously feed upon the acts and feed energies into them. In the process, the victims become brutalized and are likely to subsequently manifest similar low vibration levels. Through this process, criminality breeds further criminality. There are no winners.

In some lifetime or another, someone probably rode over the hill and ravaged you and yours. Well isn't turnabout fair play? Aren't you justified in ravaging the ravagers if you get the chance? Not unless you wish to perpetuate "an eye for an eye" in an endless vicious cycle! At coarser vibration levels, turnabout is *not* fair play—it is just collective madness.

In our transition times, we hear much about crime as a major social problem, and it is certainly an unpleasant part of the current social scene. However, there has been progress from earlier historical spirals. It is now safer to travel across the United States or through Europe than it was a century ago. The cities of industrialized nations are safer than they were in earlier times. Money is safer in banks than it was in previous eras. Socrates and Jesus would not be executed today. Nor would King Henry's wives go to the tower and the headsman.

When criminality is viewed from this slightly higher perspective, some surprising things are uncovered. The media tend to focus our attention on street crime—violent acts committed here and there. However, the greatest perpetrators of crime have been, and still are, governments themselves. Those who are not "of the tribe," or at least staunch allies, are fair game. In pursuit of their own ideological or economic policies, most modern governments have laid waste the lives and properties and environments of other countries. These are surely crimes against humanity, whatever the justification. The United States' and Russia's biggest kill counts in Vietnam and Afghanistan, respectively, were civilians. In *Global Mind Change*, Willis Harman reports that in World War I, approximately 15 percent of the casualties were civilian; in World War II, over 50 percent were civilian; and in the Vietnam War, close to 90 percent were civilian. Who says all is fair in love and war?

Another surprise is that "white-collar" crime, that is, crime committed by corporations and their executives, is far more costly than street crime. The U.S. Justice Department estimates that white-collar crime costs $200 billion a year— *eighteen times* the estimated cost of all street crimes. About half of the five hundred leading American corporations have been convicted of at least one major crime in recent years. The number of lives lost due to shoddy equipment, illegal pollution, false inspections, and negligence is probably also much higher for white-collar crimes than for violent street crimes.

This is not to deny in any way that street crimes are hazardous and costly for everyone, but the media's emphasis on street crime leads us away from focusing on far more dangerous forms of criminality. Faulty automobiles, such as the old Pinto, and the illegal handling of pollution and toxic waste have killed many more people than cult leader Charles Manson or Son of Sam.

Many approaches have been tried in the attempt to control crime, and societies have spent huge resources in such attempts, often to little avail. Prisons may temporarily keep criminals locked away from the rest of society, but the high recidivism rates of released convicts suggest that prisons are not very successful either in rehabilitation or deterrence. At best, the modern criminal-justice system is a holding operation that helps keep the peace to some degree.

The only thing I know of that reliably and durably reduces criminality is raised consciousness. There are no hard statistics on this yet, but most observers agree that crime rates of all types (including disfiguring the human soul) are much lower among those involved in the human-potential movement. When a person has more empathic awareness of others, it is much more difficult, even personally painful, to transgress against these others or allow them to be in harm's way. Among people who believe in the laws of karma, it is particularly ethically difficult to harm others.

Criminality is not likely to entirely disappear during the upcoming spiral. Perhaps it will not entirely disappear as long as beings come to this physical plane, because there may continue to be individuals who play the paired game of oppressor and victim. However, crime, like everything else, may become more voluntary and more isolated—a curiosity rather than a threat for those who don't wish to play.

White-collar crime is already becoming more unacceptable. Defense-contract frauds, insider trading, massive consumer rip-offs, and so on, are not new, but the rising hue and cry against them is. Government crime may be the hardest to curtail, but world opinion is even becoming less supportive of this.

If we could fully trust our fellow humans, our corporations, and our governments, it would be a new historical spiral indeed.

Chapter 26

DEVIANCE

Not so long ago, anyone who deviated very much from the prevailing values and standards of his or her group was in grave personal danger. A person could very easily be persecuted, ostracized, or killed for holding the wrong political or religious views, for supporting the wrong cause, for having the wrong sexual desires, or even for looking different. One could be ruined by being falsely accused of such things, even if one were entirely innocent.

Who is deviant? Several years ago, in a widely cited study, I asked this question of several hundred midwesterners from all walks of life. The results were rather astonishing. The responses included hundreds of different characteristics. The usual categories were there: homosexuals, radicals, druggies, and so on. However, the list also included college students, Democrats, Republicans, women drivers, intellectuals, girls who don't wear makeup, know-it-all professors, Jesus freaks, smokers, people who believe the Bible, people who *don't* believe the Bible, extra-smart people, psychologists, Unitarians, and television watchers. (A rather conventional friend of mine found himself on the list fourteen different times.)

It seems that just about everything most of us think, feel, and do is considered deviant from *somebody's* perspective.

Conversely, virtually everything most of us currently agree is deviant has been the prevailing practice in some location during some historical time period. For instance, Westerners commonly regard incest as deviant, but brother/sister marriages were routinely practiced by the royal families of ancient Egypt and Hawaii. Also, the mothers of one South Sea Island tribe soothed their fussing infant sons by orally manipulating their genitals. Examples of the cultural *relativity* of deviance are endless. The catalogue of "strange customs" from around the world is flatly mind-boggling.

Deviance is customarily defined as a violation of the major norms and standards of a group or society. The more rigid a group's standards, the sharper the dividing line between conventionality and deviance. Nothing is "naturally" deviant; deviance is always relative to some set of standards held dear by those doing the judging. Deviance is thus always in the eye of the beholder.

Since people are always intensively programmed with the standards of their group, they tend to shy away from violating any of these standards themselves, and they tend to condemn the violations by others. This is a powerful form of social control of group members, and it is a powerful manifestion of prevailing mass thoughtforms. Some of this may be "good"; it helps to keep the group together through the sharing of values and prevailing thoughtforms. However, the cost is high. In the past, this mechanism has created an incredible amount of human misery. It has also stifled the human spirit.

One major effect of rigid moral standards is that they have caused a great many people to sharply separate their private selves from the public images they feel they must maintain. Whatever their private thoughts and behaviors, they present an edited, conventionalized public version of themselves that they hope will be acceptable to their fellows. If they are party to thoughts, feelings, or activities that violate the local standards, they often suffer feelings of guilt and shame. Many people, when such thoughts arise, fervently repress them to the best of their ability.

Rigid standards have caused multitudes of people to be secretive, to feel guilty, to repress themselves, and to "pass" publicly for normal. Again, some of this is "good" in that it keeps people from committing murder, selling out their companions, or impulsively engaging in self-destructive behavior. However, especially in earlier historical spirals, this was almost always overdone, to the point that social control became heavy-handed social oppression.

The human psyche is far larger and more multidimensional than any group's worldview and set of standards. Therefore, rigid values and beliefs can straitjacket full expression of the human spirit. For instance, trying to fit the total human being into a single gender stereotype—male or female—is like trying to stuff a three-dimensional object into a two-dimensional plane.

Standards of normality and deviance have often been used by zealots of one stripe or another to justify ruthless persecutions and purges. So, along with guilt and repression, people who have been involved in deviance have also often experienced free-floating anxieties and fears, with good reason. This has further motivated them to remain "in the closet" and has also made them overly cautious and wary of their own inner natures. This can be a devastating form of self-estrangement.

This intermix of guilt and fear has caused personal anguish for hundreds of millions of people and has curtailed their free-flowing openness with others. Legions of boys and girls have suffered self-doubts because they have masturbated. Other people have wondered about their sanity because they have had spiritual experiences that diverged from the prevailing local religious doctrines. Huge numbers of people have feared to voice their private opinions publicly. Women who have simply enjoyed sex have worried about whether they were "nymphomaniacs." More people than one could number easily have been afraid of showing physical affection toward members of their own gender. The majority of whole populations have "behaved themselves," "kept quiet," and "done what they're told." The result is *a tyranny of the prevailing mass thoughtforms.* This is one sense in which an incarnation can be viewed as an imprisonment. It is also a way in which we must free one another in order to truly free ourselves.

Over the years, I have done research on a number of different types of deviants, from drug users and mystics to flower children and ex-convicts. In all of this research, one thing always emerged: Deviants are human beings. However, they are human beings with two sets of problems. First, they have the same problems as anyone else currently on the physical plane: getting their teeth fixed, paying taxes, buying groceries, and so on. Additionally, they have the problems of managing their divergence from the prevailing standards, in the face of a disapproving society. One solution they have is to seek associations with kindred spirits. However, deviants must still get jobs and rent apartments and so on. So the insulation from the rest of society can never be complete. Whether their deviance is "major," such as radical politics, or "minor," such as intellectualism in a redneck community or pot smoking in Texas, they move through a psychic field of rejection, contempt, and disgust. Even if they successfully lead secret lives, they will hear disparaging jokes about "their kind." If their deviance becomes publicly known, there may be a show of tolerance, but their families and acquaintances are likely to mount "reform efforts." The New Ager may have darkly admonishing quotations from the Bible sent to him or her; the homosexual male may be introduced to interesting girls; the Bohemian intellectual may be invited out for beer and baseball.

Deviance should not be romanticized. As with any large

segment of humans, the ranks of deviants contain beings currently manifesting as "nice people" and beings currently manifesting as "not nice people," but they are not the scourge of God, as some television preachers have presumptuously asserted. The vast majority of deviants are just plain folks who march to a different drummer. Also, today's deviants are not infrequently tomorrow's pioneers or saints.

Deviants can cause trouble. We fear that certain types of deviants may seduce our children into wayward ways or bring harm to ourselves and those we love. However, we can well harbor these same fears about military leaders and corporation executives, who also provide us with threats. The vast majority of deviants are only *different.*

Organizations, administrators, and officials are interested in keeping the peace (as they see it), so they tend to define deviants as "boatrockers": rambunctious children, cutting up teenagers, whistle blowers, smart asses, and troublemakers. However, as a great many people have remarked, some boats need to be rocked. Remember that a full list of deviants includes Marie Curie, Nelson Mandela, Lech Walesa, Gauguin, Mozart, Susan B. Anthony, Socrates, and Jesus of Nazareth.

A good many of the people aligned with modern social transformation feel a bit deviant because they embrace paradigms considered outlandish, if not dangerous, by much of the prevailing society. Some live somewhat "double lives," while others take some risks by going public. They seek solace by networking and associating with kindred spirits, but many I know are haunted by the "loneliness of the long-distance runner." Their physical, financial, social, and spiritual supports are sometimes quite marginal when compared with those of their more conformist acquaintances.

There is a common frustration among these social transformers of feeling that they know some of the secrets of the universe, but they are not always able to communicate these uplifting secrets to those around them. Sometimes they chew their fingernails, pluck at their hair, or seek massages or other bodywork to assuage the stress of these frustrations. I suspect that these souls may be the true heroes of our transition times.

In our transition times, the lines between conventionality and deviance are beginning to blur. The shackles of rigid standards are falling away. In practical terms, what this means is greater freedom of expression for people with respect to religion, sex, political views, lifestyles, and all other areas of physical-plane living. There is a rapid proliferation of alternative "little worlds" of beliefs and behaviors that people can choose among—a cafeteria of choices.

There is a historical shift from people being considered deviant to people being considered just different and a growth in tolerance of other people's ways. An attitude of "You do your thing and I'll do mine" is becoming the norm. This transformation is far from accomplished yet, but it will be one of the prevailing characteristics of our future lives. It involves replacing tribal morals with ethics based on more universal spiritual principles such as those stated in the Declaration of Human Rights.

Such a transformation, even if only partial, will lead to a widespread lessening of guilts and shames and fears, an increase in interpersonal openness, and greater freedom to choose our own ways and walk our own self-designed paths.

"Free to be, you and me. . ."

Chapter 27

RELIGION

Religion has, in one manifestation or another, been the constant companion of humanity throughout its evolutionary adventures. Although much distorted by humans, it has been the expression of transcendental spiritual truths on the physical plane. It has also been a source of direct spiritual experiences. However, the history of religion is a very convoluted one because humans have been very active (and often overactive) agents in its representation, administration, interpretation, and perpetuation.

There has always been an intermix of the divine and the human, the transcendent and the earthly, in religion. For this reason, specific religions have always partly reflected whatever historical spiral in which they have manifested. This perennial intermix of "above and below" is what has made the study of religion so fascinating and so convoluted.

Some form of religion has existed in every known society. It has been a part of life in each succeeding historical spiral, although its role has often been very different in every one. In the early Hunting and Gathering Spiral, humans were closely intertwined with living nature, and there was little or no separation between the spiritual and the mundane in the consciousness of the people. Everything from communing with the spirits of wood, stream, and animal to cooking a meal and engaging in sex had a simultaneous sacred and physical focus. This was a style of living so qualitatively different from that of most modern urban people that it is hard for most of us to conceive of unless we connect with resonances from our own distant past. Ideas such as "the conquest of nature" would have seemed ridiculous and perverted to these ancient people. They knew how to *sing* to nature and exist within its living bosom. In the Gardening and Herding Spiral more elaborate rituals developed, but spiritual experiences were commonly deep and direct.

As the Agricultural Spiral came into prevalence, the dominant religions of the previous spirals underwent very significant changes. In effect, the "natural" religions of the earlier spirals, with their spiritual symbolization of the elements, were taken over by a priestly caste of people who were usually in political cahoots with an area's rulers. Spirituality was "interpreted" for the masses of people by these "priests" in ways that reinforced and justified the stark political and economic inequalities of the times. These priests actually did hold a great deal of knowledge and power in their hands, so they were able to demonstrate the "righteousness" of these positions. During this period, elaborate dogmas arose that were crafted from an intermix of inspiration and zealous or self-seeking expediency.

Then along came a few vaulting, advanced spiritual masters: Jesus of Nazareth, Gautama Buddha, Zoroaster, Lao Tzu. Their infusion of vaulting spiritual truths into the human psyche has been reverberating down through the centuries, although the echoes have become muffled and distorted through human tinkering.

These new spiritual infusions were at first strongly resisted by most of the officials and priests. However, their truth and strength was too much to entirely repress, so as they took root and flowered, parts of these teachings were co-opted by the established ministries. The prevailing religions thereafter became highly organized, with the priests designated as the only official channels to spirituality and the only arbiters of doctrine. Common people needed priests to guide them. Dogma was the law of the land. There were, of course, some spiritually advanced and compassionate priests, but they themselves were not infrequently purged as wayward, heretical, and disobedient. However, the original spiritual infusions were so vaulting and so powerful that, despite all these human machinations, strong glimmers of truth remained.

The people usually kept some of their own spiritual traditions, which were sometimes tolerated as "strange local customs" but were more often brutally repressed by the religious officials. If you knew where to go, there would be an esoteric fringe, frequently in the form of secret societies, in which practices and beliefs above and beyond the state religions were taught and preserved. Some of these, such as Wicca and the Gnostic Christian tradition, are only coming out in the open again during our own time.

In the story of religion there is a grim paradox. Religion stems from humanity's basic spiritual nature, and it is found everywhere. Yet holy wars and persecutions have, in earlier spirals, been the most cruel and bloody forms of human violence. As only one example, between the fifteenth and seventeenth centuries over half a million people were burned at the stake by Christian zealots. This apparent paradox is resolved if one grasps the fact that organized religions are *human organizations*. As such they reflect, at least to some degree, the prevailing imbalances, dark energies, and exaggerations of the historical spirals and societies in which they have roosted.

These human organizations have usually been the keepers of the scriptures and have therefore been the source of human editing. A spiritual teacher might say, "Those who do not heed their own inner urgings to master their lower selves may find themselves returning in the next life as much animal as

spirit." Several generations later, a zealous priest from the ruling class might "interpret" this scripture as "Those who do
not obey their masters will find themselves returning in the
next life as an animal." Or the spiritual leader says, "Those
who deny their own and others' spirituality will suffer a self-
created darkness that may seem everlasting until they see the
Light." With fierce human editing this might become "Those
who transgress against the Holy Spirit will suffer everlasting
Hell." (Today's channeling of spirit guides has a similar danger of human editing.)

As the Industrial Spiral came into prevalence, the basis of
mainstream religion became a matter of *accounting*—the
balance of debit and credit accounts in some great ledger in
the sky (with columns for sins, penance, good deeds, and
redemption). Spirituality became more distant and abstract.
Western religions sharply divided creation into the sacred and
the profane, the worldly and the other-worldly. Extroverting
one's attention onto the physical environment was emphasized. Introspection, which had been the hallmark of sages
and mystics, came to be viewed as a mark of emotional instability ("Snap out of it!") if not mental derangement.

In later stages of the Industrial Spiral, there was a marked
decline in the force of religion in the world. Such notables as
Freud, Marx, Darwin, and Bertrand Russell saw religion as
something of a childish superstition that "man" would outgrow as civilization advanced. Science and rationality would
replace such superstitions.

Belief and direct spiritual experience dwindled, and so
did involvement in religion. Those who held religious convictions (as the majority did) compartmentalized them off from
the rest of their lives. Rather than being a living, intrinsic
ingredient in all human activity, religion became a Sunday-
morning social and a nice idea. But one didn't allow it to
interfere with the real-world "affairs of men."

Distant and compartmentalized, religion could then serve

as a justification for almost anything. Perhaps the zenith of this trend was the following famous quotation of Adolph Hitler: "Who says I am not under the special protection of God?"

During the twentieth century in industrialized countries, there has been a decline in weekly attendance and size of offerings in *established* religious denominations. However, the notables who predicted the demise of religion couldn't have been more wrong. What has occurred instead has been a *change* in religion over the last three decades that has gone hand in glove with other social changes.

In our transition times there has been a ground swell of two religious vectors: fundamentalism and New Age spirituality. At first glance, this may be puzzling because the two would seem to be at opposite ends of the spectrum, but in fact they have more in common than is usually realized and more in common than either fundamentalists or New Agers are usually willing to admit.

Both camps embody an awareness of the spiritual nature of humans, and both believe in the importance of things spiritual for meaningful living. Both reject the status quo because of its gross dominance of the material pole over the spiritual pole. In both fundamentalism and the New Age movement, there is an emphasis on the availability of *live*, direct experience of spirituality and the energizing power of spiritual images, so that religion can become an intense personal experience again rather than an abstract belief. Both encourage individuals to live in the Light if they wish to handle and rise above their turmoils and problems. Spiritual awakening is seen by both as the only real and lasting way to turn around a troubled life.

There are, however, also marked differences between the two camps. In some respects, fundamentalism is a backlash movement that seeks a return to the more stringent principles and practices of earlier historical spirals. Most fundamentalists, for instance, assert that the Bible is inerrant—literally true, word by word—despite the mounting archaeological and historical evidence that it has been massively edited and tinkered with over the centuries, as have all sacred scriptures. Fundamentalists also perceive modern society as corrupt and libertine—like the whore of Babylon. They are also part of the backlash against feminism. For these reasons, fundamentalists tend to strongly support ultra-conservative, right-wing political causes and candidates. They also put down the worldwide spiritual awakening and human-potential movements as dark, blasphemous trafficking with malevolence—a position that echoes the religious persecutions by zealots so common in earlier historical spirals.

As part of the broader human-potential movement, the spiritual-awakening camp stresses direct realization of one's own spiritual essence and the raising of one's spiritual awareness and abilities. It does not rely upon any priesthood or centralized organization, and in fact feels that these can be more limiting than supporting. For example, in Chelsea Quinn Yarbro's *Michael's People*, Michael asserts, "Where a teaching limits choice, it is more dogma than enlightenment." Each individual is seen as an *active agent*, a co-creator, in the spiritual manifesting and evolvement of the entire living cosmos. In this view, we are not spiritual dependents but independent coauthors. In *Eye of the Centaur*, veteran metaphysician Barbara Hand Clow expresses this idea: "When we mature and grow we mature and grow God, and when we pollute and kill we pollute and kill God." Insights, images, and techniques from all of humanity's diverse religious and mystical traditions are freely borrowed in the construction of a *personal* recipe that is intentionally fluid. One learns from others, but ultimately one is one's own priest.

Like so many veteran mystics, Sri Swami Rama warns us, in *Choosing a Path*, to sharply distinguish between religion and spirituality:

There is a vast difference between religion and spirituality. A religion is a set of dogmas, doctrines, and rituals. A student of religion is not allowed to think or search beyond these sets of rules. But in spirituality, all the human resources are directed toward the search for the spirit only—the ultimate Truth. A spiritual human being can be religious, but a religious human being is not necessarily spiritual.

The rapid worldwide growth of this meta-religious spirituality is the biggest religious news of our time. During the 1960s and 1970s, an intermediate stage of this growth occurred: the appearance of a host of different cults with both Eastern and Western roots. In their heyday, these cults probably had hundreds of thousands of members, but by the mid-1980s they had waned, and they continue to decline in numbers and influence. Members often found some spiritual truths and experiences within their confines, but most of these cults became progressively authoritarian. Many were wracked with internal scandals of one sort or another, such as the personal aggrandizement of the leaders and financial rip-offs. Many cult leaders also eventually became egomaniacal beyond belief. Ex-members have frequently reported they simply outgrew them. One ex-member I know, who had donated large sums of money and worked almost a decade in one of the major cults, laughed and said, "Easy come, easy go."

A primary feature of the new spirituality is the use of empirical rules of evidence and the scientific method to explore and verify spiritual phenomena and the paranormal. Scientific procedures are also being used for the development and refinement of consciousness-expanding techniques. Studies have been done on near-death-experiences, out-of-body experiences, past-life experiences, streamlined yoga and meditation techniques, mechanical devices for synchronizing right-brain and left-brain functions, the collection and preservation of native mysticisms from around the world, photographing the human aura, and the unearthing and deciphering of ancient manuscripts that are part of humanity's religious heritage. At the forefront of these investigations is a new and very modern breed of human— people trained in both science and mysticism. All indications are that this trend is only in its infancy; its eventual implications are almost beyond imagining. For certain, it will change the face of religion. People are getting less distorted, more "objective" views of "the real story" of life on this planet and in the mul- tidimensional cosmos, and are even mapping the Beyond. The data keeps pouring in, and in the long run it cannot be denied.

Since much of the Earth is still embroiled in the manifesta- tions of earlier historical spirals, we can expect to see traditional sectarian religions continue to exist for some time. However, as people's general awareness level rises, we can also expect to see some fading of divisive sectarianism, and perhaps the replace- ment of self-righteousness with simple spiritual awareness that is compassionate and tolerant of the paths of others.

The overwhelming majority of writers on this subject see the twenty-first century as spiritual. The details of such a prevailing spirituality might be fantastic indeed. They might include rou- tine communications between the physical plane and the Beyond, as Robert Monroe has suggested. Training in creative visualization, meditation, and the releasing of negative emo- tions might become an accepted part of public education, as Louise Hay has hoped. Couples planning to marry might have the synchronicity or abrasiveness of their auric fields electroni- cally tested. In times to come, we will know a great deal more about the true history of our planet and of the cosmos. We can expect a continuing movement away from organized, institu- tionalized religion and toward individual, personal spirituality. And "religion" may become not a matter of faith, but of direct experience.

We have busy lifetimes ahead.

Part Three
THE
UPLIFTING

The whole history of scientific advance is full of scientists investigating phenomena that the Establishment did not believe were there.

MARGARET MEAD

The only effective and permanent way to change the world in which we live is to change our level of consciousness.

KEN KEYES, JR.

If the mind can heal and transform, why can't minds join to heal and transform society?

MARILYN FERGUSON

Next lifetime you will do it differently anyway, so why not do it differently right now.

LOUISE HAY

A little while, a moment of rest upon the wind, and another woman shall bear me.

KAHLIL GIBRAN

Only through the eyes of your soul can you know the impact of your life upon mankind.

ORIN / SANAYA ROMAN

Chapter 28

LEADING
EDGES

A large, complex society is never an entirely monolithic or unified system. As it moves along in history, it always has some leading edges, trailing edges, and side trips. Acclaimed sociologist Herbert Blumer has found this sort of spread, for example, in the rise of new fashions, a process that involves innovators, early adopters, the majority, and laggards.

The edges or fringes of society are always minority themes within a mainstream. They are "unofficial," that is, they are hardly represented, if at all, within the official structures and institutions of the culture. However, they are very often where the action is, historically speaking. They are also harbingers, in rudimentary form, of things to come. History has demonstrated again and again that today's fringe is tomorrow's prevailing mainstream belief and practice.

In ordinary times (if there are such things), only a small fraction of a society's population gets involved with fringe activity. These fringe members are the discontented, the restless, the social casualties of one kind or another, and the seekers. They are usually held in rather low esteem by the solid citizens and sometimes tolerated, sometimes oppressed, by the ruling officialdom. However, those whom conventional people laugh at and belittle—early Christians skulking in the catacombs of Rome, public-education advocates, food faddists, early rocket inventors—may be generating things that become a taken-for-granted part of the lives of their children and grandchildren. The fact that a particular fringe group is small in numbers means nothing; it still may subsequently have vast historical influences, unguessed by anyone in the early stages. If we are presently lending our support to some leading-edge movement that seems discouragingly small, we must take heart; the historical evolvement process may be running our way.

New thought forms, lifestyles, beliefs, and technologies usually arise first at the edges of societies or civilizations—almost never within their conventional Establishment centers. If successful, these new forms subsequently penetrate into the mainstream culture, eventually altering its shape and collective spirit. This successful penetration can be recognized and verified therefore by changes in the prevailing mass thought-forms. This is the process through which have arisen the great religions of the world, the giant political systems, and most major institutions such as public education, the criminal justice system, social welfare, and suburbia, as well as the Planned Parenthood League and the United Nations.

Ordinarily, during the fairly stable periods of a historical spiral, the fringes are a fascinating but minor key in the goings on. But during the transition times into a new evolutionary spiral, the fringe "heats up." Many more people become involved, and there is a tumultuous whirlwind of experimentation with alternative forms and ideas. In fact, this flurry of fringe activity is one of the most reliable signs that a transition time is occurring for real. For example, such flurries of activity occurred during the transition into the Agricultural Spiral and again during the transition into the Industrial Spiral. New religions and philosophies, new paradigms about human nature and the cosmos, and new lifestyles (all condemned by the trailing edges) sprang into being. Such a flurry is also happening on many different fronts in the world today. There are a multitude of individuals and groups thrashing about in their desires and yearnings to break out of the old forms. At a certain point, a critical threshold is reached, and the leading-edge activity reaches a pitch that births *some* kind of new epoch. This is inevitable and unstoppable. From all the evidence at hand, our modern culture has already passed this threshold.

It is my experience that new-wave movements, buoyed up by their enthusiasms and sense of fellowship, almost always underestimate the entrenched strength of the inertia and barriers they face. So they are often disheartened. However, it is also my experience that the old guard *always* underestimate the restless strengths of the new waves eroding their edifaces, and they are amazed when the new historical wave comes to prevail.

Leading-edge developments are usually experimental, and often fumbling. They are not always successful in themselves. However, they "stir things up" and help break apart the old forms, and they are subsequently built upon and refined by others. A good recent example of this was the events of the 1960s. A lot of people became involved at that time in an amorphous movement to change the way things were. The drug activity certainly didn't work very well, and there were some casualties from this and other sources. However, the events of the 1960s boosted the peace movement, the women's movement, the human-potential movement, and the movement toward freer sexual expression. American life was changed forever.

In our own times, there is a clamorous array of leading edges straining forward toward a new era. Altogether, they total dozens of different movements, many thousands of different organizations and groups, and tens of millions of people throughout the world. Many of these movements are presently unacquainted with and even unaware of one another.

They represent a bewildering variety of different beliefs, jargons, hopes, and causes. They may also be in conflict with each other, but these squabbles are *irrelevant* in the larger scheme of things. All of these movements are bringing a new spiral into existence. *They are all actively shaping our future lives and the circumstances that will surround them.* Their individual and small-group actions interface and converge, knowingly or unknowingly, to form a major historical wave of monumental proportions. This is really the bottom-line answer to the question "What's going on?"

There are a few very broad leading-edge movements. They do not encompass all that is going on, but they do give a suggestion of modern society's thrust and direction. A great many people are involved in these movements without even fully realizing it—for example, the publisher who no longer accepts sexist writing from authors, or someone who joins Amnesty International, or a person who passes an interesting book about New Age spirituality to a friend is involved. Millions of such daily actions become a landslide of millions of votes for a new world.

The academic term for these kinds of broad historical thrusts is "social movements," but this term can be misleading because it suggests that they have more cohesion and organization than they actually possess. They more nearly resemble collective tropisms or synergistic wave fronts. Following are some of these broad fronts that are pushing our history forward and creating the beginnings of qualitative changes.

LEADING-EDGE SCIENCE

Leading-edge scientists come from all scientific backgrounds and are almost always involved in research rather than teaching or administration. They are in love with new ideas. Being on the forefront of their sciences, they are a bit unconventional and disreputable in the eyes of their more conventional colleagues. They tend to be rowdy, irreverent, and visionary, but they keep winning Nobel Prizes and National Academy of Science awards. They crop up on Public Broadcasting System interviews and documentaries. They are venturesome and passionate, and they see science as somewhat heroic. They like mavericks, such as Einstein, and they like to contemplate far-fetched notions.

These scientists dream of bright technological futures for humanity: space colonies, undersea cities, ocean farming, genetic engineering, unlimited energy sources. A number of them write science fiction on the side and a great many of them read it. There is something of a diffuse international kinship and conspiracy among them that often leaps political boundaries.

Leading-edge scientists are often at odds with the conventional scientific Establishment and its pedantic conservatism and old-world, mechanical theorizing. This tension sometimes shows up as exasperation in their writings. As Einstein said, "Great spirits often encounter violent opposition from mediocre minds." In *Life Between Life*, Joel Whitton, M.D., Ph.D., wrote; "Despite the success of Darwin in abolishing God from Nature, of Freud in reducing the divinity of [humanity] to the need to suck on a breast, and despite the supreme achievement of the Behaviorists in extinguishing consciousness, the belief in something beyond death persists."

There is also an impatience with science when it is practiced merely as a ritual instead of as an imaginative adventure. The eminent social scientist Peter Berger said, "In science, as in love, a concentration on technique is quite likely to lead to impotence."

The new scientists are busy building the technological platform for the upcoming historical spiral, and they are in the process of transforming humanity into a space-faring species. Although they are rigorous in their research, they tend to be very impatient with fixed ideas and the other barriers examined in this book. *They want a new world.*

Their numbers are relatively small, so they are usually a minority within their own sciences. Because their research is unconventional, they usually must scrounge for financial support even after they have achieved acclaim. The big grants usually go to their more conventional colleagues, but the breakthroughs usually come from the leading-edge scientists. They are the pioneers. They will get us to the stars.

THE HUMAN-RIGHTS MOVEMENT

In 1948 almost all the nations of the world signed a Universal Declaration of Human Rights that could certainly stand as a political platform for the next evolutionary spiral. Since that time, not one of these countries has even come close to living up to the declaration's tenets. However, it has been a standard and a rallying point for an unprecedented worldwide human-rights movement, the likes of which has never been seen before.

Within this broad movement are many diverse currents: various civil rights movements, hunger relief, the women's movement, the Peace Corps, Amnesty International, and so on. There is a growing world opinion that cries "foul" to the worst atrocities against humanity and that pushes for some degree of equal rights and equal opportunities for all humans. Historically, there have always been atrocities. The difference in modern times is (1) everyone usually knows about them more quickly and (2) there is much more collective condemnation for them than in previous epochs.

One interesting aspect of this movement is the large number of rock music superstars who have become human-rights troubadours: Bruce Springsteen, Peter Gabriel, Sting, Tracy Chapman, U2, Bob Dylan, Willie Nelson, Phil Collins, Dire Straits. . .the list goes on and on.

The human-rights movement has done a great deal to raise the collective awareness and conscience level of the world. Things that were just a part of life in earlier historical spirals, such as mass exploitations and mass killings or the repression of whole segments of populations, are now becoming atrocities in the court of world opinion. Along with the desire to eliminate, or at least curtail, such negative activities, the human-rights movement is pushing for a positive shift in human conditions. For instance, many individuals and groups are helping people in Third World countries with more productive agricultural techniques, low-level medicine, and education. This in itself is not enough to transform the lives of the three billion underprivileged members of humanity who are stuck struggling with the first levels of Maslow's hierarchy of needs: shelter, water, subsistence. However, the growth of the widespread idea that such needs should and could be met is most promising for all of our future lives.

Members of this wave front have focused most intensely on rebalancing the self-interest / collective-interest polarity. Many understand the basic insight expressed so well by nineteenth century English poet Edward Carpenter: "One's soul is in touch with the souls of all creatures." Human-rights workers realize that human development is collective as well as individual. The goal of basic civil rights and subsistence services for all humans is still far from being achieved, but decade by decade, tremendous progress is being made.

Overall, there has been an uneven but unmistakable increase in human rights as humanity has worked its way through the historical spirals. Most signs promise that, in the upcoming era, basic human rights will be more secure than they have ever been before.

THE ENVIRONMENTAL MOVEMENT

The Industrial Spiral that we are now in the process of transcending has been noted for many positive inventions and human betterments, but its energies and imbalances have also had a ruthless and rapacious impact upon the Earth's biosphere. Ecological balances have gone "tilt' in our time, to the point where humanity's life-support systems are in jeopardy. Spaceship Earth is being fouled by its crew.

In the last few decades there has been a rapid growth in the concern over many aspects of our physical and social environments. According to the July 28, 1989, Public Broadcasting System program "Washington Week in Review," the percentage of the U.S. population concerned about the environment had risen from 3 or 4 percent thirty years ago, to over 70 percent by 1989. Part of the concern is over the immediate external and internal environment of human bodies. The Surgeon General of the United States, the Sierra Club, Greenpeace, the Green political parties in Europe, the National Wildlife Federation, *Prevention* magazine, consumer protection groups, and nutritionists, to name just a few, are all concerned with the health of the Earth and its creatures, including humans. Their aim is to increase public awareness of environmental issues and to get legislation enacted and *applied* that provides for some regulation of destructive technological activities.

Many people are still only vaguely aware of environmental issues, unless their lives have been personally touched by, for example, toxic spills in their hometowns. Also, so far, most politicians have only been making public-relations statements in attempts to soothe and quiet the environmental agitators. There have also been numerous confrontations between elements of this movement and elements of business and industry who do not wish to be curtailed in their actions. The mass thoughtforms of the Industrial Spiral (involving humanity conquering nature) are still so strong that the public is difficult to fully arouse with respect to the environment. Therefore, business often still has things its own way, despite the outpouring of rhetoric. Most of the world shrugged, for example, when the French government blew up a Greenpeace vessel protesting a nuclear test, and a man was killed. Meanwhile, the skies are brown instead of blue over most of the world's major cities.

The environmental movement involves a fundamental shift in human focus from regarding the environment as a *target* to be controlled and manipulated to regarding the environment as a living, sovereign entity that is the source of life on this planet and that humanity should respect, honor, and cooperate with. This basic shift also involves a greatly expanded perceptiveness of the living environment, its rhythms, and its energies. Humanity's direct experience of the living environment can be a real spiritual revelation. Aside from anything else, this "with nature" viewpoint enriches living, and, to put it baldly, it is probably going to be necessary for our survival.

The environmental movement is an especially grassroots one, involving large numbers of "ordinary people" with many different viewpoints and allegiences. Because this wave front addresses keen self-interest issues of survival, it is likely to become the largest and most-talked-about movement over the next few years. Even people who have little concern for human rights or far-fetched science or spirituality become concerned when their immediate lives are threatened.

It has become obvious to virtually everyone working in this area that, in order to avoid ecological cataclysms, humanity must establish mutually supportive practices *with* the environment. There must be a partnership. These mutually supportive practices must extend all the way from the international level down to the individual level. This is a necessary condition for the occurrence of *any* future spiral.

The good news is that environmental awareness is rapidly growing. Also growing is the deeper awareness expressed by the visionary teacher Nicki Scully in *Your Future Lives:* "All living things that share this planet with us are our relatives."

THE HUMAN-POTENTIAL MOVEMENT

In many different forms and under many different guises, the human-potential movement or wave front amounts to a collective psychic stirring and awakening of humanity's inherent potentials. Directly or tacitly, it is mystical in its conceptions of human nature. It involves a radical break with the mechanistic Newtonian view of the universe and the objects within it. It is holistic rather than reductionistic; that is, it conceives of things as by-products of consciousness, rather than conceiving of consciousness as a by-product of things. As the early visionary Andrew Glazewski put it, our consciousness is not in our body; our body is in our consciousness.

This viewpoint is blasphemous in the eyes of conventional science and conventional religion because it transcends the basic tenets of each. However, it is likely to be the prevailing modus vivendi (way of life) of our future lives within the next historical spiral. Some writers have gone so far as to assert that either the twenty-first century will be spiritual—or there won't be any twenty-first century.

This movement is even more varied in its approaches than the others. Its range extends from the seeking of self-realization through procedures that are only one step beyond conventional psychology to the most esoteric and arcane rarified spiritual beliefs and practices. Its membership is also the most broadly based of the wave fronts, drawing upon all professions, all nationalities, and all walks of life and lifestyles. Even a partial list of the groups and approaches involved would cover many pages, but this wavefront is larger than the sum of its parts. Also, new groups and approaches continually arise and join its ranks.

There is never a perfect fit between the established structures of a society and the needs and desires of the population living within it. This is why collective behavior arises. In times of rapid change, the fit can become very poor indeed. Discontentment levels rise and people begin actively striving to "do something about it." The result is what futurist Barbara Marx Hubbard calls "evolutionary drivers," through which humanity rises to the occasion and carries out the birth of a new age.

It is as if the collective human psyche has risen to an awareness of the imbalances and failings of the current spiral. These imbalances have become progressively more unacceptable when they have denied the breadth and depth of human nature. In all the elements of the human-potential movement, there is a *yearning* that goes beyond politics or materialism. Consequently, this wave front goes beyond the others in its radical implications for our future living.

The human-potential movement is a creative fusion of a multitude of mystic traditions from around the planet, cast in contemporary images, with a seasoning of new science and maverick psychology. This movement has had to emerge from the shadows of centuries-long repression of mystic traditions by orthodox churches, the state, orthodox science, and the prevailing beliefs they fostered. But it is truly coming out now. Throughout history, older souls have kept these ingredient mystic traditions alive and have preserved them quietly. The time of their flowering has now come.

How radical a departure from prevailing conventionality is the human-potential movement? Consider this: Human beings are deathless spiritual entities, temporarily incarnated in biological bodies on the physical plane, which is only one of many dimensions of the living cosmos. Behind, beyond, and beneath the various games with which people are ordinarily preoccupied is THE GAME of spiritual evolvement throughout all these dimensions. *This is what's really going on!*

In this prime game, everybody eventually wins. Also, we are all active players, not just pawns. When our spiritual wellspring is ignored or denied, parts of THE GAME become more grim and laborious. When our spiritual wellspring is recognized and connected with, THE GAME becomes a lighter dance with more thrills and fewer chills. Either way, we are attending Earth school, gathering experiences and learning lessons. We "work it out" both individually and collectively. There are "vacations" during in-between lives in the Beyond. But we "do the course" until we graduate to other stages of THE GAME. The more advanced "students" help the less advanced, as an inherent part of their own further evolvement.

As Barbara Hand Clow has pointed out, "Once we realize we return to Earth again and again, once we see this, it will be impossible to destroy the home we return to" (personal correspondence).

Not all those in the human-potential movement would buy this entire mystical perspective *yet*, but it is inherent, if not yet manifested, in most of their work and strivings. Nor can this perspective be found in a Sunday-school primer or your high school science text or corporation prospectus or government brochure. However, all of these reflect the old world, not the new.

The human-potential movement includes a bewildering array of assertions, techniques, and procedures. There are biofeedback and what maverick author Robert Anton Wilson calls "mind machines" to alter states of consciousness and brain-wave rhythms. There are mystic herbalism and nutrition drawn from Chinese medicine and tribal shamanism. There are many forms of meditation and yoga. There are various sorts of Christian and Jewish mysticism that were formerly underground. There are chanting and the channeling of advanced discarnate spirits. There are past-life-regression therapies. There are creative visualization, positive affirmations, and techniques for the releasing of past resentments, phobias, and addictions. There are exercises for changing deep-seated beliefs. There are disciplines for producing out-of-body experiences and astral traveling. And there are exercises for connecting with one's Higher Self and Universal Intelligence. However divergent all of these might seem, they have a common premise: that there is a spiritual basis to humanity and the cosmos. They also share a common aim—an increase in human awareness and consciousness. The collective vision shared by the human-potential movement is the *spiritual awakening of humanity.*

In *The Aquarian Conspiracy*, Marilyn Ferguson has expressed the underlying feeling of this wave front: "What counts is that something in us is wiser and better informed than our ordinary consciousness. With such an ally within our Selves why should we go it alone?" Or, as New Age therapist Edward Sparks said in *Your Future Lives*, "If you want to meet your Saviour, try looking in the bathroom mirror." Or as the channeler Iris Belhayes put it, "Everything we do is spiritual, no matter how it seems." In the introductory sentence of *Global Mind Change*, futurist Willis Harman challenges us: "If the world that science tells us about is *reality*, how does it happen that we don't feel more at home in it?"

A great many people have found the return of a sense of wonder and excitement within the human-potential movement, a *coming alive*, to replace their previous stresses and routines. Some critics have castigated those involved for being self-indulgent and self-interested at a time when the world stands in crisis, but this criticism shows their own lack of comprehension about what is actually going on here. Those involved in the human-potential movement naturally (rather than dutifully) become more actively concerned with human rights, the environment, and the beneficial use of technology. They also manifest higher, more positive vibration levels in their daily lives. For example, most observers agree that crime rates of all types against persons or property are unmistakably much lower among New Agers.

The mass media apply the catchword "New Age" to this entire wave front. This may serve as a convenient term, but it in no way captures all that is going on. Also, media discussions using this term are often distorted, focusing on the more glitzy, superficial, and bizarre facets of the human-potential wave front. "New Age" is also becoming a marketing label for new commercial products and advertising gimmicks. We can expect to soon see New Age breakfast cereal with carob-coated cherubs and pyramids, and a New Age sex manual.

The human-potential movement differs sharply from other movements, such as revolutionary struggles, that try to solve particular problems but so often only end up being interchanges of negative energies. The thrust of this movement is, instead, to *outgrow* a great many of our current social problems. From even a partly raised collective consciousness level, situations such as wretched leadership and gross economic distortions might disappear. For example, in most late industrial countries, an overt position of racial prejudice or military aggrandizement is already political suicide for any candidate. Most of us, as we have grown from childhood to adolescence to full adulthood, have had the experience of outgrowing some of our problems and hang-ups and inadequacies. It is reasonable to expect a similar progression for the human race as a whole.

No single specific thrust, such as Save the Whales or the Peace Corps or a New Age publishing company, stands much of a chance alone to make a transforming impact on the world because of the inertia and barriers of mainstream societies discussed earlier. However, *thousands upon thousands of such thrusts,* linked by new era images, cannot be ignored or withstood for long.

It is a very good bet that these four broad movements will have more to do with our future lives than anything else happening on the planet today.

All four of these wave fronts have actually been around for a long time, during earlier spirals, in more subterranean, rudimentary, and "fringie" forms. However, it is only during our transition times that they have shown a widespread surge.

It seems almost as if, in the evolutionary game, the forms that will prevail in later historical spirals are worked out in proto-type by the individual and collective psyches of earlier spirals. If this intriguing idea is true, then some of the prototypical forms for the spiral *beyond* the upcoming one are lurking around somewhere already.

Chapter 29

"UNFINISHED BUSINESS"

History does not repeat itself. But far too often we humans find ourselves seeming to repeat ourselves. This is because we are sometimes locked into patterns of perception, emotions, and actions from previous times. We find ourselves almost hypnotically repeating these patterns, like scripts we compulsively perform again and again to the point of utter weariness. We may even get to thinking that these repetitive patterns are "the way we are" and "the way things are" rather than recognizing them as just unreleased compulsions. It would be more useful for us to think of these patterns as "unfinished business."

Also, we often find ourselves locked into repeating certain kinds of relationships. For example, we may have fights with a parent, child, or lover during which we catch ourselves hurling the same remarks at one another year after year. Or we may go through a tiresome series of work, friendship, or romantic relationships that look rosy at first and then turn sour. Whenever the words "always" or "never" are attached to such interpersonal patterns, there is unfinished business. (For example, "I'm always disappointed" or "I'm never appreciated.")

When we look beyond ourselves and our own personal relationships into the wider spheres of community, society, and world, we begin to see a lot more unfinished business. Doing something about the problems within these wider spheres is not just a nice idea to make us feel good about our charitable impulses. The fact is that, wherever we are going, we all go together.

Looking at our major institutions, such as the school system, organized religion, business, the medical establishment, and government, we find a heavy residue of collective images and patterns from earlier historical spirals and earlier phases of the Industrial Spiral. An analogy could be made with our basements, attics, and garages, where a lot of "stuff" has accumulated over the years and is waiting to be sorted, cleaned out, or disposed of. If we don't do this, the debris eventually becomes cloying. We could drown in our own refuse. Our accumulated debris represents a blight upon the physical, social, and spiritual landscapes.

At the level of society's major institutions, there is often more unfinished business than we can easily face up to. Our technology enriches us with one hand and imperils us with the other. Our school systems dull our minds and our souls, even as they provide windows on the world. Our mass media link the world, but they pander to the lower chakras and leave the higher ones begging. Our political systems consist mostly of rule by special interests, and they routinely rob our checkbooks, with little more than empty rhetoric in exchange. Our economic systems feed and shelter us, but they are houses of cards that leave us restless in our sleep. Our organized religions promise salvation but tie us up in spiritual knots. The medical establishment rapes our bodies with gleaming instruments and charges us exorbitant fees for the experience.

However, we continue to sift and sort and learn and grow, and we continue to become more autonomous and self-reliant. You can't keep evolving spirits down.

The quality of services we receive and the user-friendliness of our social institutions are what is in question. The fact that they are much better than ever doesn't vanquish the fact that they are not good enough to support a truly uplifted life for the human race.

At the level of nations, there are many countries that have still not even fully uplifted into the Industrial Spiral, and their statistical profiles demonstrate the fact. For instance, in industrialized countries, the infant mortality rate is under 12 per thousand; in developing countries like China, it is five times as great; and in largely undeveloped nations like Pakistan, it is over ten times as great (125 per thousand). There is a great deal of other data that tells a similar story. Per capita gross national product in industrial nations is over eight thousand dollars per person, while in India and Kenya it is less than *one twenty-fifth* of this amount. These figures indicate that most people in nonmodernized countries are still struggling with the lower levels of Maslow's hierarchy of needs: food, water, shelter, and minimal safety.

At the world level, humanity has the unfinished business of establishing a true symbiotic relationship with planet Earth rather than being a parasitic infestation upon its surface. There has been an estrangement between Mother Earth and much of humanity that needs to be healed.

And there is the unfinished business of the pollution of the "nearby" lower astral planes. Almost every old house, every ancient battlefield, every marked or unmarked graveyard, is inhabited by earthbound spirits emanating lower vibrational wavelengths and lost in their own psychic fog. The low astral levels are teaming with spiritual derelicts who add their darker colorations to Earth's psychic atmosphere. These vibrations form part of our collective atmosphere, and they can affect us the same way as any septic environmental situation.

All this personal and collective unfinished business is the cause of an energetic pattern that has puzzled many people. Peak experiences and transcendent moments are often fol-

lowed by crashes. Feeling good and happy is too often followed by not feeling good and not being happy. What happens is that old negative patterns, old interpersonal habits,
and bad news coming in from our web may bring us down
and produce feelings of despair and hopelessness. We think,
"Is it ever going to change?"

As we look around, we can see "unfinished business" on
every hand. The real question is, how do we finish it? How do
we escape from merely perpetuating it?

Given our current individual and collective situations,
conventional approaches can make our problems seem insoluble. Using current methods, *they probably are.* But wait!
Throughout history, problems that have been insoluble in
one historical spiral have been easily resolved with the
increased knowledge and technology of the next spiral. For
instance, in 1820 the average American farmer could grow
only enough to feed 4.7 people beyond his or her own family,
so huge cities were impossible. With mechanization and
other technical advances, the average farmer can now grow
enough to feed 48 people—a tenfold increase. Before the
high-speed printing press, mass education was impossible;
before the development of the assembly line, mass transportation was impossible. Without the massive increases in all
forms of mobility, our current increased freedom from rigid
traditions would not be possible.

Therefore, some of the "unfinished business" of a particular epoch can be cleaned up only with the more advanced
technology, knowledge, and collective thoughtforms of a later
epoch. However, *beginning* to clean it up hastens the birth of
the new epoch and significantly smooths the transition.

In our current times, at the personal level there is a similar
phenomenon at work. Young people often cannot get decent
paying jobs until they get formal educational training.
Ordinarily, they cannot successfully be "on their own" until
they approach adulthood. This is an example of how we often

experience reruns of problems and non-optimum situations until we are able to change our level of consciousness.

Willis Harman delineates the simple but profound mechanism involved in these changes, and also points out the importance of the broad movements examined earlier: "Throughout history, the really fundamental changes in societies have come about not from the dictates of governments and the results of battles, but through vast numbers of people changing their minds—sometimes only a little bit."

Releasing the accumulated psychic debris of the human race is an "everybody wins" game because the accumulation is both individual and shared. Each release of debris makes further releases easier because all the individual "strands" are interwoven and shared by the whole human race. Historical novels, war stories, horror movies, and dark-tale novelist Stephen King yarns are ingested by multitudes, perhaps as fumbling attempts to "safely" contact and release the "stick-em," as Chris Griscom calls it, of past spirals. In *Heart of the Christos*, Barbara Hand Clow suggests that all the past lives we've ever lived on this planet are being replayed in the movies and on television. Certainly, these earlier times have provided enough plots and raw material for the tales. However, the human-potential movement is providing better, more reliable ways of undertaking such contact and release, as discussed in Louise Hay's *You Can Heal Your Life*, and Richard Gerber's *Vibrational Medicine*.

Will we make it to a new spiral? Happily, the odds are overwhelmingly in our favor. It is a virtual certainty that we will. Any one of the factors discussed in this book—loosened bonds, increased voluntarism, heightened awareness—*virtually guarantees a brighter new era.*

The compassionate religionist Lewis Timberlake has a nice saying: Failure doesn't mean we're failures; it just means we haven't yet succeeded.

Chapter 30

MAKING IT

So here we are, individually and together, on the threshold of our future lives.

It would be nothing but presumptuous to assume that we know the *details* of what's going to happen in the next century or even in the next few years. The details, such as which party will capture the U.S. presidency or where the stock market will be or whether we will experience inflation or recession, belong to the topmost, superficial level of change, and they are being continually rewritten by the interweaving of our individual images and actions. Detailed predictions don't work very well because we keep revising our scripts as we go along.

Nor can we be very sure about predictions regarding the second level of change—the infrastructure of society and the prevailing routine patterns of living. For instance, it would be risky to bet on whether more or fewer people will seek advanced education degrees or whether the middle class will shrink or expand a bit in the near future. Also, we are unlikely to foresee the development of specific technical devices and the influences they might have on the rest of society.

Arthur C. Clarke, the famous scientist and science fiction writer (*2001*), wrote a brilliant article entitled "The Hazards of Prophecy." In it, he analyzed the various predictions people had made over the years, looking for why they had often missed the mark so badly. He found two factors involved in their failures. The first was a *failure of nerve*. This involved a lack of boldness on the part of the prophets. They saw the future as being like the present, only a little more so or less so. Even with the evidence before them, they failed to draw the proper conclusions because of their fixed considerations— much like current mainstream scientists who deny all of the accumulated data on the paranormal. The second factor was a *failure of imagination.* Here the would-be prophets failed at "thinking the unthinkable." They could not imaginatively anticipate "surprising" developments. They were unable to conceive of major technical and belief-structure shifts that arose and resulted in qualitatively different living experiences for humans on the physical plane. In both of these failures, the forecasters were too caught up in the thoughtforms that prevailed in their own times and places.

Using knowledge of the deepest tidal level of change, it is possible to escape both of these failures to some extent. These deep evolutionary tides are somewhat inexorable, which is why they are very likely to carry us through the changes, even in the face of some disasters. They are that strong, resting as they seem to be on the entire evolving collective human psyche. This fact doesn't wash away all of our present aches and pains and worries, but humans surmount catastrophes better than is sometimes realized. As a recent example, both Germany and Japan were bombed into rubble during the Second World War, but twenty years later they were grabbing off some of the U.S. market share of product after product and financing much of the U.S. mounting national debt. As another example, many of us know individuals whose lives have been in ruins at one point but who have been doing all right again a few years later. However bumpy the road ahead, there will not be a fallback to earlier historical spirals. Humanity won't have to invent arithmetic or guitars again.

So what do we have going for us, individually and collectively, to get us over the thresholds that lead to a higher spiral and more beneficent future lives? A great deal, actually. We have everything necessary to succeed:

- **All the powerful positive trends examined in this book.** Taken together, these add up to a veritable avalanche of evolutionary thrusts *uplifting* us into a higher spiral. As transition people, we are riding the crest of these waves. We may get a bit wet now and then, but we won't go back.

- **We have the long-term accumulation of *positive karma* and all the lessons we have already learned along our evolutionary path.** In other words, we have the built up "bank account" of all our previous accomplishments, stored in our libraries and in our souls. Once any physical-plane lesson has been learned, it is ours forever and is able to enrich all subsequent lifetimes. Even if there were widespread disasters at the mundane social level, very little technology would be lost. The basic knowledge is too widely distributed throughout the world. For instance, we would not lose the technology of aspirin or automobiles or eyeglasses, or the plays of Shakespeare, the techniques of meditation and yoga, or the teachings of Seth. There are billions of textbooks and reference manuals extant in the world. Also, most of humanity's original inventors and developers have probably incarnated back onto the planet again. As each decade passes, the human race grows individually and collectively wiser.

Based upon information from mystic literature, it seems that, at about the beginning of the Industrial Spiral, more older souls began to incarnate on planet Earth. The pivotal point would seem to have been around two or three centuries ago. From all the evidence, older souls *tend* to be more empathic and less prone to create havoc for themselves and those around them. They are also prone to be more spiritually awake, so they will gradually swell the ranks of the human-

potential movement. There will be an increasing proportion
of older souls with each passing generation. This means that
every year, no matter what else is happening in the world,
there is further spiritual evolvement of the human race. The
implications of this are simply wild.

- **We have the very impressive creativity and intelligence of
  "ordinary people."** It has often been fashionable to disparage
  ordinary people because, for example, they don't know who
  Kierkegaard was or where the Sea of Cortez is located. In
  doing extensive field research on many different social worlds,
  I have again and again been struck by the abilities of ordinary
  people to fashion stable lives out of whatever they find in their
  physical and social environments. Given even half a chance,
  the majority of people will put together some sort of life that
  works and will get something accomplished. This is a *crucial*
  factor, because the story of any given spiral, and any transition
  into the next, is the story of *all* the inhabitants, not just the
  famous figures or the esoteric fringes. We all grow together.

- **We have a motivation toward the future.** Freud, Darwin, and
  other old-world theorists have misled us in many ways. One of
  them has been the erroneous notion that we are shaped and
  motivated only by past influences and factors. In fact, people
  are also motivated by the future, like children striving to grow
  up who socialize and train themselves for future manifestings.
  Millions upon millions of people are now yearning and
  actively striving toward a more beneficent future. As they take
  steps in that direction, changes begin to occur in the world's
  holographic psychic fields. As the fields "lighten up," it then
  becomes easier for others to reach toward a brighter spiral of
  tomorrows, so this future-oriented process becomes self-
  perpetuating. This process also produces an increase in the
  incidence of spontaneous paranormal phenomena.

  There is something else at work here that seems quite mysterious but powerful. Probable futures seem to somehow
  actively enlist the aid of certain persons in the present, in
  some psychic manner, to act as midwives in their coming birth.

Many people have remarked, often with puzzlement, that they have been "recruited" to help bring some future pattern into manifested reality. Are these recruitments "pulls" from future selves that are calling to us, as Seth has intimated? I don't know, but I do know that many people have felt such pulls. One person said, "It's like the Grail is looking for *me*."

- **We have our zest for life.** Yes, there are many negative energies abroad in the world that color our auric fields, but there are multitudinous emanations of positive, life-affirming energies too. We like to give and receive and share life energies. All over the world, people plant flowers and nurture pets and celebrate affirming holidays, no matter what else is going on. This collective positive thrust has carried us through thick and thin, through our darkest hours, and through a host of natural and human-made calamities during all the preceding historical spirals. Human beings have demonstrated that they are very good at picking up the pieces. Surveys have shown that springtime is the favorite season for the majority of humans. Like the Persian poet Omar Khayyam said,

> Come fill the cup and in the fires of Spring,
> Your Winter garment of repentance fling.

- **We have the hierarchy of more evolved spirits who act as benefactors and well-wishers of humanity.** Without interfering with our own free will, these more advanced souls help us with our uplifting and evolvement. They seem to aid us in many subtle and direct ways, such as providing inspiration and being guides for those departing physical life. Most of these discarnates have gone through and transcended the human experience themselves, so they know what it's all about. They "return to the old neighborhood," so to speak, to lend a hand. It seems that one of the things more advanced spirits routinely do is help and succor less-evolved beings. Evidently, this is an inherent aspect of their own further development.

Highly evolved spirits have also provided the answer to a

question that has haunted many people: What if we don't make it? What if, through nuclear madness or some other environmental disaster, the story of the human race on Earth is aborted while yet unfinished? The unanimous reply of the guiding spirits is that we would be "resettled" someplace else to continue and complete our evolvement. No doubt this would entail horrendous travail and shock, and grief beyond measure. It would be a long road back to overcome and transcend the knowledge that we *killed our planet*. However, the point is that "the end" really wouldn't be the end at all; we'd have other chances, other places. The notion of eternal damnation is a social control mechanism, not a cosmic truth.

- **We have love.** We usually think of love as a very personal thing—something we do late at night with a breathless partner. Or a feeling that wells up inside us toward our children when they are especially cute or especially hurt. Or a diffuse feeling we have about a pet until it knocks over our favorite vase. Or a fleeting heart twinge over a story of personal misfortune in the media. It may also be the momentary "recognition" of another soul, like a brilliant photoflash that leaves afterimages.

   But the Teachers tell us that love is also a great social and spiritual force in the universe, like a cosmic wind that blows everywhere and is the strongest force of all.

   I don't understand love very much yet myself; I'm still just a pup in the evolutionary scheme of things. Now and then I almost see it out of the corner of my eye. Or I catch a faint sense of it like a distant song I almost hear. I suspect that it's all around me on the higher planes and that I'm not unlike someone fast asleep in the midst of a carnival. But we're all waking up.

   In *Michael's People* (Chelsea Quinn Yarbro, scribe), Michael says that the experience of evolution is the gradual triumph of love over fear. "Love has endured in the face of every sort of criminality, catastrophe, annihilation or other comprehensive 'disaster' known anywhere on the physical plane," he says. "Nothing in the universe is stronger than love, or more enduring."

The most fundamental conflict in the universe is evidently *not* between good and evil or between darkness and light, but between fear and love.

We gaze into the undiscovered country of the future and half glimpse some of its wondrous possibilities. But since we have not yet experienced the transmutation, we cannot perceive it too clearly. As physicist Peter Russell has pointed out, how can a water molecule know what it's like to be a steam molecule? However, with our knowledge and foresight we do have some inklings of where we're going.

There will no doubt be mechanical and technological wonders for us in the upcoming spiral. Far beyond any of these, however, will be the experience of being in on the collective spiritual awakening of the human species. This should prove to be an awesome experience indeed! It will not happen uniformly throughout the planet. More likely it will spread outward from spiritually awakened "pools," until the pools link together to form expanding swirls. There will still be "kinky" things going on, but they will more frequently occur by conscious mutual consent.

What will future historians have to say about our era? They will probably be gently amused by us—the curious, half-asleep, half-awake people who were living at the dawn of *their* spiral. We will be seen as the fascinating transition people, who lived as much by our obsessions and fixed ideas as by our truths, who played complicated hide-and-seek games with our own essential natures, who played Russian roulette with our environment—and who dreamed of something better. The threshold people. But we can gently smile, too, because those future historians will be ourselves. The conversation might go like this: "I didn't recognize you for a moment in your new body."

The great English poet Alfred, Lord Tennyson once wrote, "'Tis not too late to seek a better world."

Waiting for us up the evolutionary spiral in our future lives is all the adventure we have ever longed for, all the sex we have ever wanted, all the companionships we have missed, all the aliveness and beauty that we can bear, and all the possibilities necessary for the realizations of our secret dreams.

Hey—let's go!

EPILOGUE
Stepping toward the Future

Scientific analysts, mystics, and "ordinary people" have all, almost unanimously, come to the conclusion that we are at a time of crossroads in our history. In addition to the fact that this conclusion seems almost universal, there are two other crucial things about it.

First, we are at a great multitude of crossroads, not just a single one. This is perhaps always true of transitions, because living beings and societies are themselves multifaceted. To put this another way, a major transition always has a-thousand-and-one facets, or historical pressure points, just as the human body has a multitude of physical pressure points.

From this point arises the crucial second one. In the process of our daily living, we have continuous *choices* regarding many of these historical pressure points. What causes do we contribute to? In what direction do we steer the conversation during lunch? What do we say, or refrain from saying, to others about current events? How do we spend our leisure time?

With regard to these many crossroads, individuals and groups make millions upon millions of choices in the process of living. The choices that are made stem from the basic predispositions, of those doing the choosing. Change the predispositions, and you change the choices made. Change the choices made, and you change the world and our future lives.

For the last few years, I have been doing field research, examining the characteristics of people actively involved in working toward a new era. My conclusions are still very preliminary and tentative, but a general pattern of predispositions in these people seems to be emerging. Because the conclusions are still tentative, they can be treated only as such, but with this proviso, they can serve both as an interim report and a possible recipe for anyone wanting to contribute to the birth of a new age and its prevailing character.

This profile and "recipe" of predispositions seems to arise in response to the basic question "How do we get from Here to There?" The question also implies the fervent hope of getting from Here to There with as few unpleasantries as possible.

This recipe shouldn't be taken too seriously. Because each individual is, in some respects, unique, the contributions of each individual will be unique. If you have the desire to assist in the conscious creation of a brighter future, your own intuitions are, in the long run, the best guide.

Even though each person's path has unique features, the generic predispositions that follow are usually present among those assisting in the birth of a new spiral. These predispositions are not static attributes; they are dynamic tropisms. To emphasize this, they are presented in the ". . . ing" active verb form.

LEARNING

Finding out what's *really* going on is obviously valuable in order to make positive choices, but this is not always easy to do. One often has to step outside of ordinary channels to find out what's really happening because of the tunnel vision that tends to prevail in conventional mainstream sources. Becoming informed usually involves "piercing the veil" of superficial data and entrenched belief structures. New-era people routinely spend some time and energy doing this.

Two trends are, however, making it easier to be well informed. One is the rapid growth in the availability of nonfiction paperbacks. One must pick and choose among them, but they are the best single source of data and insights about our transition times and where they might be heading. The other trend is the documentary programming that is becoming increasingly available on basic cable television. Again, one must pick and choose, but the fare available in the U.S. on public broadcasting stations, the Discovery channel, and CNN contains news and special features that are usually more penetrating and unconventional than mainstream media. There are also many magazines devoted to specific facets of the emerging changes, such as *OMNI, Vegetarian Times, Yoga Journal, Spectrum,* and *Body, Mind & Spirit.*

New-era people learn a good deal from one another. The learning can involve both the gathering and updating of knowledge and the gaining of skills relevant to our transition and a new era. It also involves *fluidity:* holding one's appraisals and conclusions very lightly, and being ready to change them on the basis of new inputs. The following are a handful of books that explore the overall patterns of our transition times and give many hints of future possibilities:

Capra, Fritjof. *The Turning Point.* New York: Simon and Schuster, 1982.

Ferguson, Marilyn. *The Aquarian Conspiracy.* Los Angeles: Jeremy Tarcher, 1980.

Harman, Willis. *Global Mind Change.* Indianapolis: Knowledge Systems, 1988.

Hubbard, Barbara Marx. *The Evolutionary Journey.* San Francisco: Evolutionary Press, 1982.

Russell, Peter. *The Global Brain.* Los Angeles: Jeremy Tarcher, 1983.

Schindler, Craig, and Gary Lapid. *The Great Turning.* Santa Fe: Bear & Co., 1989.

Simmons, J.L. *The Emerging New Age.* Santa Fe: Bear & Co., 1989.

Yarbro, Chelsea Quinn. *Messages From Michael.* New York: Berkley, 1979.

For those desiring a more in-depth examination of many of the topics discussed in the preceding pages, I recommend Ian Robertson's *Sociology,* and Parrillo, Stimson, and Stimson's *Contemporary Social Problems* (see Bibliography).

GROWING

A growth in awareness is one of those wonderful games in which everyone wins. It must be emphasized that such expansion of awareness is not just a left-brain, intellectual "sharpening of one's mind." The keen analytical mind has been worshiped during the last couple of centuries, but it has proven to be utterly inadequate and sterile by itself. New-era growth involves expansion of the whole person, including the right brain, heart, and spirit.

The growth attempted by new-era people can be both very mystical and exceedingly practical. The mystical aspects of growth involve an increase in inner self-realization and spiritual awakening, although these may be expressed differently in different jargons. The practical aspects involve an increase in health, success in daily living, and a switchover to more positive outlooks and emotions.

Both aspects increase self-independence and personal freedom (inner-directedness). Personal growth can, and usually does, produce some growing pains—temporary disorientations, upsets, and interpersonal flare-ups. However, the expanded, lighter, more positive mode that is attained through this growth is, to put it simply, more adventurous and more fun. Everything around one, from machinery to foliage to other beings, also usually benefits. Each changed individual changes the collective hologram of humanity. Here again, one must chart one's own personal path, but there are a great many noncoercive techniques available to help.

In pursuing personal growth, it is wise to be wary of any group or cult that seeks to "capture" individuals more than free them. There are three main danger signs to look for: (1) the group charges huge sums of money (growth need not be financially ruinous); (2) the group idolizes some human leader (break the habit once and for all of kneeling to others); and (3) the group condemns other spiritual paths or self-realization techniques and claims to be the only way (this is usually a coarse-vibration-level social control tactic, and everyone who's been around knows there are many paths).

There is also a glitzy, superficial level of the New Age movement that is not very helpful. It involves either promises to ascertain one's fate (rather than help one create it) or promises to aid one in manipulating others. Both these kinds of promises violate universal spiritual principles.

The books listed earlier contain much data on personal growth; in fact, it may be impossible to learn without growing. Here are a few more books that a great many people have found very helpful:

Gawain, Shakti. *Creative Visualization.* New York: Bantam, 1978.

Hay, Louise. *You Can Heal Your Life.* Santa Monica: Hay House, 1984.

Roman, Sanaya. *Personal Power Through Awareness.* Tiburon, CA: H.J. Kramer, 1986.

Silva, Jose, and Robert B. Stone. *You the Healer.* Tiburon, CA.: H.J. Kramer, 1989.

Vande Kieft, Kathleen. *Innersource.* New York: Ballantine, 1988.

MOVING

New-era people display a predisposition toward being on the move. This moving can take many different forms: physical, psychological, interpersonal, social, and spiritual. Moving through our transition times and into our futures can involve any or all of these. A premise of both new science and ancient mysticism is that the cosmos is in continuous flux. Therefore, a predisposition toward mobility would seem necessary in order to stay "with it." This appears to be a common attribute of those who are successfully dealing with the times and contributing to them in a positive manner.

Moving involves a kind of courage; it involves trusting the unfolding of evolution and one's intuitive sensing of this unfolding. The reward for such courage is that one is far less likely to be caught flat footed when times change and change again. Conversely, stubborn resistance to flux seems to produce disharmonies and abrasions.

Moving one's possessions from one locale to another is an apt analogy for this predisposition. In a physical move of this sort, one sorts through possessions, streamlines them, discards some things, adapts other items to the new location, and gets new things for a new ambience.

Being ready and able to move on fairly short notice is part of this basic tropism. On the basis of voluminous research findings, even mainstream psychology is coming around to viewing the Self as a fluid, dynamic pattern of processes rather than a static structure of traits.

Those who change their minds, their hearts, their careers, and so on, are sometimes regarded as "fickle" by those who are staunchly committed to the old ways. In fact, however, moving seems to be an individual and collective successful adaptation to changing times.

SEEKING

This predisposition often appears as simple restlessness, but this perception misses the fact that it is restlessness with a purpose. Seeking is a self-motivated searching for alternative paths, channels, and ways. It stems from a basic dissatisfaction and disagreement with the status quo, arising from increasing awareness. Restless populations are not appreciated by the Establishment, but they are the creators of change.

Seeking can have the down side of occasional discontentment and frustration. It isn't always fun, and it can be a lonely endeavor at times. However, for a great many people, it is a healthy alternative to tranquilizers or apathetic resignation, and it often embodies the zest of exploration and questing. It often uncovers routes to transformation and transcendence. It is future oriented—it encourages an attitude of scouting ahead.

Seeking may be narrow gauge, as with someone searching

for more egalitarian relationships or nondrug methods for handling stress. Or it may be more generalized, as with someone questing for new-era alternatives in virtually every aspect of their lives. Either way, the people involved are *looking for something;* they are alert to new and different possibilities. They are the ones who think about the unthinkable and contemplate doing the outlandish. They often go ahead and do it.

Exploring far-fetched alternatives is a somewhat "disreputable" activity, but as time goes on, the fantastic often become the usual. The fact that so many people are currently seeking alternatives is strong support for the premise that we are indeed in the midst of transition times.

CONNECTING

In some manner or other, new-era individuals are predisposed to connect up with other vectors that are threading their way through our times toward a brighter new spiral. This may be formal, as when one joins some of the organizations involved with the four broad wave fronts examined earlier. It can also be informal, as when one makes the acquaintance of a few similar-minded people in one's locale or votes for the more environmentally committed candidate. This formal and informal connecting results in a great deal of networking among new-era people.

Connecting can also be an inner process, occurring within the mind, heart, and spirit of an individual. Based on Rupert Sheldrake's work on morphogenetic energy fields and Seth's comments on mass thoughtforms, these inner connectings should not be discounted nor their influences underestimated.

This predisposition always involves disconnecting from old-world patterns and allegiances. Such withdrawals can create upset and consternation, as when people cease supporting mainstream organizations or a wife ceases to tolerate a patriar-

chal family style. At the collective level, multitudes of individual
connectings and disconnectings add up to societal withdrawal of
support for old-world patterns and the swelling of support for
new-era ones.

In *Global Mind Change*, Willis Harman demonstrates that
such collective shifts in connectedness can be crucial because the
ultimate power of any major institution stems from the degree to
which people grant it legitimacy. Or withdraw legitimacy from
it. Without such granted legitimacy, a political, economic, or
military institution becomes a withered husk and is replaced by
something else.

PROPAGATING

New-era people tell others about their predispositions, discoveries, and exploring of alternatives. Thus, these rudimentary
new patterns spread or "diffuse," as anthropologists say, from one
individual, group, or nation to another.

New-era people give talks on environmental issues to luncheon clubs; someone loans a New Age book to an acquaintance;
rock stars promote Amnesty International and Greenpeace; Bernie Siegel gives an interview on the spiritual aspects of healing in
a major woman's magazine; a scientist tells a congressional committee about the high frontier of space and permanent space
colonies; a friend tells a friend. . .This is propagating.

The mathematics of these propagations are both fascinating
and important. If one person who is connected into some facet
of the new era disseminates information to just one other person
per month, then twelve more people are educated that year. If
each (or some) of these twelve then disseminates information to
one other person per month, and so on, there is an exponential
curve that amounts to an epidemic contagion.

The active manifesting of these predispositions in a multitude
of ways by tens of millions of people adds up to a smoother passage through our transition times and into a brighter future. As
Tennyson said, "'Tis not too late to seek a better world."

APPENDIX

UNITED NATIONS UNIVERSAL DECLARATION OF HUMAN RIGHTS

Article 1
All human beings are born free and equal in dignity and rights. They are endowed with reason and conscience and should act towards one another in a spirit of brotherhood.

Article 2
Everyone is entitled to all the rights and freedoms set forth in this Declaration, without distinction of any kind, such as race, color, sex, language, religion, political or other opinion, national or social origin, property, birth or other status.

Furthermore, no distinction shall be made on the basis of the political, jurisdictional or international status of the country or territory to which a person belongs, whether it be independent, trust, non-self-governing or under any other limitation of sovereignty.

Article 3
Everyone has the right to life, liberty and the security of person.

Article 4
No one shall be held in slavery or servitude; slavery and the slave trade shall be prohibited in all their forms.

Article 5
No one shall be subjected to torture or to cruel, inhuman or degrading treatment or punishment.

Article 6
Everyone has the right to recognition everywhere as a person before the law.

Article 7
All are equal before the law and are entitled without any discrimination to equal protection of the law. All are entitled to equal protection against any discrimination in violation of this Declaration and against any incitement to such discrimination.

Article 8
Everyone has the right to an effective remedy by the competent national tribunals for acts violating the fundamental rights granted him by the constitution or by law.

Article 9
No one shall be subjected to arbitrary arrest, detention or exile.

Article 10
Everyone is entitled in full equality to a fair and public hearing by an independent and impartial tribunal, in the determination of his rights and obligations and of any criminal charge against him.

Article 11
1. Everyone charged with a penal offence has the right to be presumed innocent until proved guilty according to law in a public trial at which he has had all the guarantees necessary for his defense.
2. No one shall be held guilty of any penal offence on account of any act or omission which did not constitute a penal offense, under national or international law, at the time when it was committed. Nor shall a heavier penalty be imposed than the one that was applicable at the time the penal offense was committed.

Article 12
No one shall be subjected to arbitrary interference with his privacy, family, home or correspondence, nor to attacks upon his honor and reputation. Everyone has the right to the protection of the law against such interference or attacks.

Article 13
1. Everyone has the right to freedom of movement and residence within the borders of each state.
2. Everyone has the right to leave any country, including his own, and to return to his country.

Article 14
1. Everyone has the right to seek and to enjoy in other countries asylum from persecution.

2. This right may not be invoked in the case of prosecutions genuinely arising from non-political crimes or from acts contrary to the purposes and principles of the United Nations.

Article 15

1. Everyone has the right to a nationality.
2. No one shall be arbitrarily deprived of his nationality nor denied the right to change his nationality.

Article 16

1. Men and women of full age, without any limitation due to race, nationality or religion, have the right to marry and to found a family. They are entitled to equal rights as to marriage, during marriage and at its dissolution.
2. Marriage shall be entered into only with the free and full consent of the intending spouses.
3. The family is the natural and fundamental group unit of society and is entitled to protection by society and the State.

Article 17

1. Everyone has the right to own property alone as well as in association with others.
2. No one shall be arbitrarily deprived of his property.

Article 18

Everyone has the right to freedom of thought, conscience and religion; this right includes freedom to change his religion or belief, and freedom, either alone or in community with others and in public or private, to manifest his religion or belief in teaching, practice, worship and observance.

Article 19

Everyone has the right to freedom of opinion and expression; this right includes freedom to hold opinions without interference and to seek, receive and impart information and ideas through any media and regardless of frontiers.

Article 20

1. Everyone has the right to freedom of peaceful assembly and association.

2. No one may be compelled to belong to an association.

Article 21

1. Everyone has the right to take part in the government of his country, directly or through freely chosen representatives.
2. Everyone has the right of equal access to public service in his country.
3. The will of the people shall be the basis of the authority of government; this will shall be expressed in periodic and genuine elections which shall be by universal and equal suffrage and shall be held by secret vote or by equivalent free voting procedures.

Article 22

Everyone, as a member of society, has the right to social security and is entitled to realization, through national effort and international co-operation and in accordance with the organization and resources of each State, of the economic, social and cultural rights indispensable for his dignity and the free development of his personality.

Article 23

1. Everyone has the right to work, to free choice of employment, to just and favorable conditions of work and to protection against unemployment.
2. Everyone, without any discrimination, has the right to equal pay for equal work.
3. Everyone who works has the right to just and favorable remuneration ensuring for himself and his family an existence worthy of human dignity, and supplemented, if necessary, by other means of social protection.
4. Everyone has the right to form and to join trade unions for the protection of his interests.

Article 24

Everyone has the right to rest and leisure, including reasonable limitation of working hours and periodic holidays with pay.

Article 25

1. Everyone has the right to a standard of living adequate for the

health and well-being of himself and of his family, including food, clothing, housing and medical care and necessary social services, and the right to security in the event of unemployment, sickness, disability, widowhood, old age or other lack of livelihood in circumstances beyond his control.

2. Motherhood and childhood are entitled to special care and assistance. All children, whether born in or out of wedlock, shall enjoy the same social protection.

Article 26

1. Everyone has the right to education. Education shall be free, at least in the elementary and fundamental stages. Elementary education shall be compulsory. Technical and professional education shall be made generally available and higher education shall be equally accessible to all on the basis of merit.

2. Education shall be directed to the full development of the human personality and to the strengthening of respect for human rights and fundamental freedoms. It shall promote understanding, tolerance and friendship among all nations, racial or religious groups, and shall further the activities of the United Nations for the maintenance of peace.

3. Parents have a prior right to choose the kind of education that shall be given to their children.

Article 27

1. Everyone has the right freely to participate in the cultural life of the community, to enjoy the arts and to share in scientific advancement and its benefits.

2. Everyone has the right to the protection of the moral and material interests resulting from any scientific, literary, or artistic production of which he is the author.

Article 28

Everyone is entitled to a social and international order in which the rights and freedoms set forth in this Declaration can be fully realized.

Article 29

1. Everyone has duties to the community in which alone the free

and full development of his personality is possible.

2. In the exercise of his rights and freedoms, everyone shall be subject only to such limitations as are determined by law solely for the purpose of securing due recognition and respect for the rights and freedoms of others and of meeting the just requirements of morality, public order and the general welfare in a democratic society.

3. These rights and freedoms may in no case be exercised contrary to the purposes and principles of the United Nations.

Article 30
Nothing in this Declaration may be interpreted as implying for any State, group or person any right to engage in any activity or to perform any act aimed at the destruction of any of the rights and freedoms set forth herein.

BIBLIOGRAPHY

Author's note: Much of the social science research data cited is drawn from Sociology *by Ian Robertson and* Contemporary Social Problems *by Vincent N. Parrillo, John Stimson, and Ardyth Stimson (see below).*

Allman, William F. "Staying Alive in the 20th Century." *Science,* no. 85.

Bach, Richard. *Illusions.* New York: Dell, 1984.

_____. *The Bridge Across Forever.* New York: Dell, 1986.

Belhayes, Iris. *Spirit Guides.* San Diego, CA: ACS Productions, 1985.

Bell, R. "Contributions of Human Infants to Caregiving and Social Interaction." In *The Effects of the Infant on Its Caregiver,* edited by M. Lewis and L. Rosenblum. New York: Wiley, 1974.

Bernard, Jessie. *The Female World.* New York: Free Press, 1981.

Bieler, H.G. *Food Is Your Best Medicine.* New York: Ballantine, 1982.

Bohm, David. *Wholeness and the Implicate Order.* Boston: Routledge & Kegan Paul, 1980.

Brown, Lester, Christopher Flavin, and Edward Wolf. "Earth's Vital Signs." *The Futurist* (July / August 1988): 13-20.

Caplow, Theodore, and Howard M. Bahr. "Half a Century of Change in Adolescent Attitudes: Replication of a Middletown Study by the Lynds." *Public Opinion Quarterly* 43 (1979): 1-17.

Capra, Fritjof. *The Turning Point.* New York: Simon and Schuster, 1982.

Cherlin, Andrew, and Frank Furstenberg, Jr. "The American Family in the Year 2000." *The Futurist* (June 1983).

Clarke, Arthur C. "Hazards of Prophecy." In *The Social World.* 3d. ed. Edited by Ian Robertson. New York: Worth, 1987.

Clow, Barbara Hand. *Heart of the Christos.* Santa Fe: Bear & Co., 1989.

Dahrendorf, Ralf. "The End of the Labor Society." *World Peace Review* (March 1983).

Dass, Ram. *Be Here Now.* New York: Crown, 1971.

Delacroix, Jacques. "The Export of Raw Materials and Economic Growth: A Cross-National Study." *American Sociological Review* 42: 795-808.

Ferguson, Marilyn. *The Aquarian Conspiracy.* Los Angeles: Jeremy Tarcher, 1980.

Fox, Matthew. *Original Blessing.* Santa Fe: Bear & Co., 1983.

Fuller, R. Buckminster. *Utopia or Oblivion.* New York: Bantam, 1969.

Gallagher, Blanche. *Meditations with Teilhard de Chardin.* Santa Fe: Bear & Co., 1987.

Gawain, Shakti. *Creative Visualization.* New York: Bantam, 1978.

Gerber, Richard, M.D. *Vibrational Medicine.* Santa Fe: Bear & Co., 1988.

Gove, Walter, Michael Hughes, and Omer R. Galle. "Overcrowding in the Home." *American Sociological Review* 44: 59-80.

Griscom, Chris. *Ecstasy Is a New Frequency.* Santa Fe: Bear & Co., 1987.

Harman, Willis. *Global Mind Change.* Indianapolis: Knowledge Systems Inc., 1988.

Hay, Louise. *You Can Heal Your Life.* Santa Monica, CA: Hay House, 1984.

Henry, Jules. *Culture Against Man.* New York: Random House, 1963.

Herbert, Frank. *Dune.* Philadelphia: Chilton Press, 1965.

Herman, Edward S., and Noam Chomsky. *Manufacturing Consent.* New York: Random House, 1988.

Hubbard, Barbara Marx, *The Evolutionary Journey*. San Francisco: Evolutionary Press, 1982.

Hutchison, Michael. *Megabrain*. New York: Morrow, 1986.

Illich, Ivan. *Medicine Nemesis*. New York: Pantheon, 1976.

Inkeles, Alex, and David H. Smith. *Becoming Modern: Industrial Change in Six Developing Countries*. Cambridge: Harvard University Press, 1974.

Kelley, Harold, and J. Stahelski. "The Social Interaction Basis of Cooperators' and Competitors' Beliefs About Others." *Journal of Personality and Social Psychology* 16: 66-91.

Kelynda, Edward Sparks, Brad Steiger, Enid Hoffman, Nicki Scully, and Mary Devlin. *Your Future Lives*. West Chester, PA: Whitford, 1988.

Keyes, Ken, Jr. *Handbook for Higher Consciousness*. Coos Bay, OR: Living Love Center, 1975.

Kübler-Ross, Elisabeth. *On Children & Death*. New York: Macmillan, 1983.

Kuhn, Thomas. *The Structure of Scientific Revolutions*. 2d ed. Chicago: University of Chicago Press, 1979.

Lovelock, James E. *Gaia: A New Look at Life on Earth*. Oxford: Oxford University Press, 1979.

Macionis, John J. *Sociology*. 2d ed. Englewood Cliffs, NJ: Prentice Hall, 1989.

Maslow, Abraham. *Toward a Psychology of Being*. 2d ed. New York: Van Nostrand, 1968.

McCall, George, and J. L. Simmons. *Social Psychology*. New York: Free Press, 1982.

McCoy, Elin. "Childhood Through the Ages." *Parents* (January 1981): 60-65.

McLuhan, Marshall. *Understanding Media*. New York: New American Library, 1973.

Mendelsohn, Robert S., M.D. *Confessions of a Medical Heretic.* New York: Warner, 1979.

Milgram, Stanley. "The Small World Problem." *Psychology Today* 1: 61-67.

Mills, C. Wright. *The Sociological Imagination.* New York: Oxford University Press, 1959.

Monroe, Robert A. *Far Journeys.* New York: Dolphin, 1985.

O'Hare, William. "The Eight Myths of Poverty." *American Demographics* (May 1986): 22-25.

Ouspensky, P.D. *In Search of the Miraculous.* New York: Harcourt, Brace & World, Inc., 1949.

Parrillo, Vincent N., John Stimson, and Ardyth Stimson. *Contemporary Social Problems.* New York: Wiley, 1985.

Peterson, Pete. "The Morning After." *Atlantic* (October 1987).

Rama, Sri Swami. *Choosing A Path.* Honesdale, PA: Himalayan International Institute, 1982.

Remley, Ann E. "From Obedience to Independence." *Psychology Today* (October 1988): 56-59.

Ring, Kenneth. *Heading Toward Omega.* New York: Morrow, 1984.

Roberts, Jane. *The Individual and the Nature of Mass Events.* Englewood Cliffs, NJ: Prentice Hall, 1981.

_____. *Seth Speaks.* New York: Prentice Hall, 1971.

Robertson, Ian. *Sociology.* 3d ed. New York: Worth, 1989.

_____, ed. *The Social World.* 3d ed. New York: Worth, 1987.

Rodegast, Pat, and Judith Stanton, eds. *Emmanuel's Book.* New York: Bantam New Age Books, 1989.

Roman, Sanaya. *Personal Power Through Awareness.* Tiburon, CA: Kramer, 1986.

Rosenham, D.H. "On Being Sane in Insane Places." *Science* 19 (January 1973): 250-258.

Russell, Peter. *The Global Brain.* Los Angeles: Jeremy Tarcher, 1983.

Sagan, Carl. "Nuclear Winter: A Report from the World Scientific Community." *Environment* (October 1985).

Schindler, Craig, and Gary Lapid. *The Great Turning.* Santa Fe: Bear & Co., 1989.

Sheldrake, Rupert. *A New Science of Life.* Los Angeles: Jeremy Tarcher, 1982.

Siegel, Bernie S., M.D. *Love, Medicine and Miracles.* New York: Harper, 1986.

Silva, Jose, and Robert B. Stone. *You The Healer.* Tiburon, CA: Kramer, 1989.

Simmons, J.L. "Deviants." Berkeley: Glendessari Press, 1969.

──────────. *The Emerging New Age.* Santa Fe: Bear & Co., 1989.

Smith, H.W. *Social Psychology.* Englewood Cliffs, NJ: Prentice Hall, 1987.

Snow, Chet B., and Helen Wambach. *Mass Dreams of the Future.* New York: McGraw-Hill, 1989.

Stark, Rodney. *Sociology.* 3d ed. Belmont, CA: Wadsworth, 1989.

Sullivan, Thomas J., and Kenrick S. Thompson. *Introduction to Social Problems.* New York: Macmillan, 1988.

Thomas, Evan. "Peddling Influence." *Time* (March 3, 1986).

Toffler, Alvin. *Future Shock.* New York: Bantam, 1970.

Trevelyan, George. *A Vision of the Aquarian Age.* Walpole, NH: Stillpoint, 1984.

Vande Kieft, Kathleen. *Innersource.* New York: Ballantine, 1988.

Wallace, Richard Cheever, and Wendy Drew Wallace. *Sociology.* 2d ed. Boston: Allyn and Bacon, 1989.

Waters, Harry. "Life According to T.V." *Newsweek* (December 6, 1982).

Whitton, Joel, and Joel Fisher. *Life Between Life.* Garden City, NY: Doubleday, 1986.

Wilson, William J. "The Black Underclass." *The Wilson Quarterly* (Spring 1984): 88-89.

Yankelovich, Daniel. *New Rules.* New York: Random House, 1981.

Yarbro, Chelsea Quinn. *Messages From Michael.* New York: Berkley, 1979.

_____. *Michael's People.* New York: Berkley, 1988.

ABOUT
THE AUTHOR

J.L. Simmons is a renowned sociologist and field researcher who in recent years has focused on leading-edge developments and world trends, such as the human-potential movement. His best known books are *It's Happening: A Portrait of the Youth Scene Today* (a bestseller in the late 1960s), *Deviants*, and the recent critically acclaimed *The Emerging New Age* (Bear & Company).

Currently a research associate at the University of Missouri, Dr. Simmons has taught at several major universities. However, in conjunction with his longtime wife, Nola, he is now devoting more of his time to research and writing on the crucial issues facing humanity today. The Simmons family—Jerry, Nola, and sons Christopher and David—is a close one, yet, since they have studied the ways of the cat, each member is granted the space to be his or her own person.

Dr. Simmons is currently working on *Soul Mirrors*, the docudrama of an awakening old soul, as well as a book on how the human race is now poised at the dawning of a true world civilization.